Unlike the USAF or the US Navy, the US Marine Corps is a combined arms service with its own infantry, armour, artillery, special operations forces and aviation assets. All these elements train and fight together in order to conduct expeditionary and amphibious operations.

The light and manoeuvrable Marine Corps infantry specialise in assaulting from the sea and Marine Corps Aviation exists to support those troops on the ground in six ways: anti-air warfare (preventing enemy aircraft from interfering with Marine Corps operations), close air support (aka CAS – directly attacking enemy positions on the ground), aerial reconnaissance, electronic warfare, control of aircraft and missiles (battlefield command and control), and assault support (transporting troops and vehicles to the battlefield).

This book looks at the tactical jet fighter aircraft operated by the Marines since November 1947 and their increasing ability to provide support in at least two, sometimes three and now up to five of those roles.

The earliest Marine jet fighter was the FH-1 Phantom – an aircraft built in only small numbers which served mainly to pave the way for much more powerful and capable types. Its direct successor, the F2H Banshee, proved incapable of tackling enemy MiGs during the Korean War but did provide the USMC with its first fast jet reconnaissance platform.

The Banshee's contemporary, the F9F Panther, was similarly lacking in anti-air prowess but it was very successful in performing another role vital to the Marines – CAS. The Panther would become the ubiquitous ground-attack fighter of the Korean War. And radar-equipped Marines F3D Skyknights would provide new capability during the conflict as successful night fighters, despite their otherwise lacklustre performance characteristics.

After the war, the USMC would finally get full day fighter anti-air capability thanks to the later models of North American Fury, the F9F Cougar and the F4D Skyray. The latter was so

specialised as a pure inte[...]
to provide the CAS capab[...]
important for every fighter [...] the Marines.

By the early 1960s, in the face of Soviet technological advances, it was necessary to field aircraft that were just as able to hit enemy positions with bombs and rockets as they were to hit enemy aircraft with cannon or Sidewinders. The supersonic F-8 Crusader was the first Marines fighter able to truly offer this capability while also being suitable for conversion into a recon machine.

The F-4 Phantom II would take these capabilities to the next level, being better than anything in the USAF's inventory and probably the best multirole fighter in the world in its day, while the specialised AV-8A Harrier gave USMC Aviation the ability to provide CAS without runways or even a carrier deck to operate from.

Today the Marine Corps' main tactical fighter types are the AV-8B Harrier II and F/A-18 Hornet and the aircraft gradually replacing them both – the F-35 in B and C forms respectively. The Hornet is fast, reliable and carries a heavy payload of air-to-air and air-to-ground munitions. The Harrier II is subsonic and cannot match the Hornet for payload but neither does it require the Hornet's 6000m runway to carry out its missions.

But both types' days are numbered and it will be down to the futuristic F-35B and F-35C to take Marine Corps Aviation well into the 21st century. Through their advanced systems, these aircraft are capable not only of anti-air and CAS, but also reconnaissance, electronic warfare and command and control – making them a great fit for the Marine Corps of the future.

This publication chronicles the USMC's changing jet fighter inventory through the beautiful artworks of renowned aviation illustrator JP Vieira. I hope you enjoy marvelling at the incredible variety of his designs as much as I have.

Dan Sharp

ABOUT THE ARTIST

JP Vieira is an illustrator producing military history and aviation-themed artwork.

He is entirely self-taught and aims to constantly improve both the technical and artistic aspects of his work. His works combine traditional and digital methods. His attention to detail and constant pursuit of improvement makes his artworks both accurate and artistically pleasing.

JP is a published artist, collaborating with several authors, editors and publishers.

LOCKHEED MARTIN F-35B LIGHTNING II

A Marine pilot with Marine Fighter Attack Squadron 211 conducts pre-flight checks on an F-35B Lightning II aboard HMS *Queen Elizabeth* in the North Sea on October 10, 2020.
US Marine Corps photo by 1st Lt. Zachary Bodner

CONTENTS

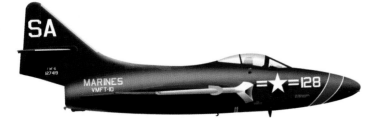

All illustrations:
JP VIEIRA

Design:
BURDA

Publisher:
STEVE O'HARA

Editor:
DAN SHARP

Published by:
MORTONS MEDIA GROUP LTD, MEDIA CENTRE, MORTON WAY, HORNCASTLE, LINCOLNSHIRE LN9 6JR.

Tel. 01507 529529

Printed by:
WILLIAM GIBBONS AND SONS, WOLVERHAMPTON

MEDIA GROUP LTD

ISBN: 978-1-911639-75-6

MCDONNELL FH-1 PHANTOM

The first jet fighter to see operational service with the Marine Corps – and the US Navy – was McDonnell's FH-1 Phantom.

MCDONNELL FH-1 PHANTOM ▼

FH-1 Phantom, Marine Phantoms aerobatic team, 1949.
An aerobatic team known as the Marine Phantoms, equipped with five FH-1 Phantoms, was formed within VMF-122. The team performed for some years and the aircraft sported this scheme, after initially flying in regular VMF-122 markings.

1947–1954

MCDONNELL FH-1 PHANTOM ▼

FH-1 Phantom, BC-1, VMF-122, MCAS Cherry Point, North Carolina, 1948.
VMF-122 became the first USMC squadron to operate jets when it received the FH-1 Phantom in November 1947.

The McDonnell Aircraft Corporation was established in 1939 to manufacture aircraft components for the United States military, its founder James McDonnell having quit his former employer, the Glenn L. Martin Company, in 1938. It turned out to be exactly the right move as huge orders soon came rolling in, but McDonnell's ambition had always been to design and build aircraft.

Therefore, during the autumn and winter of 1939, the Missouri-based company approached the USAAF with designs for a new fighter. This resulted in McDonnell being invited to participate in Request for Data R-40C on March 8, 1940 – which was for high-speed long-range bomber interceptor designs.

McDonnell's twin pusher prop-powered Model I lost out but the AAF thought highly enough of it to buy the data for $3000. The revised Model II was submitted on June 30, 1940. This also failed to attract an order but Model II-A was approved in May 1940 and McDonnell received a $1.6m contract to build its first aircraft on September 30, 1941, under the designation XP-67. This was given the company name 'Moonbat'.

This aerodynamically advanced but underpowered fighter was delivered on April 29, 1943. Early impressions were positive and it gave the US Navy sufficient confidence, on August 30, 1943, to award

the company a contract to build it a twin-engine jet fighter.

The resulting aircraft retained several of the Moonbat's features – such as its tricycle undercarriage, a pronounced dihedral of its tail surfaces, forward-set full vision canopy and the swooping curves of its faired-in engine nacelles, though the jet fighter's engines were positioned in the wingroots rather than being mid-wing.

The turbojets specified were Westinghouse WE-19XB-2Bs, each producing 1600lb of thrust. This was the first all-American jet engine and would be later redesignated J30-WE-20. Armament was a quartet of .50-cal machine guns in the nose.

The Navy ordered two prototypes under the designation XFD-1 and the first made its maiden flight on January 26, 1945, although short hops on a single engine had previously been carried out. With the type now undergoing flight testing, the Navy ordered a full production run of 100 aircraft on March 7, 1945. McDonnell continued the 'spook' theme begun with the Moonbat by calling the new aircraft 'Phantom'.

Changes for the production model would include an 18in fuselage extension, a shorter rudder and shorter tailplanes. There was also the option to install an aerodynamic external fuel tank below the fuselage and the aircraft's windscreen was redesigned to improve visibility.

The production order was slashed to 60 when the Second World War ended and the first prototype was destroyed in a crash on November 1, 1945. The second prototype became the first pure jet fighter to make an arrested landing on a US carrier – USS *Franklin D. Roosevelt* – on July 21, 1946, and the first production FD-1 made its flight debut on November 28.

Navy fighter squadron VF-17A received its first Phantom on July 23, 1947, shortly after the type had been redesignated FH-1, and the first (and only) US Marine Corps squadron to receive it was VMF-122 in November 1947. This made VMF-122 the first USMC combat squadron ever to deploy jets. And while the US Navy's Blue Angels were still flying F8F Bearcats, the Marines established their own display team called the Marine Phantoms, aka the Flying Leathernecks.

VMF-122 would also be the last active squadron left flying the FH-1, finally phasing it out on July 1, 1950. Phantoms would continue in service with training and reserve units until 1954.

The Phantom was not well suited to the USMC's requirements – lacking any ground-attack capability beyond strafing targets with its machine guns. It also had weak engines and when its guns were fired in low-light conditions they tended to dazzle the pilot. But before long much more capable aircraft would be made available.

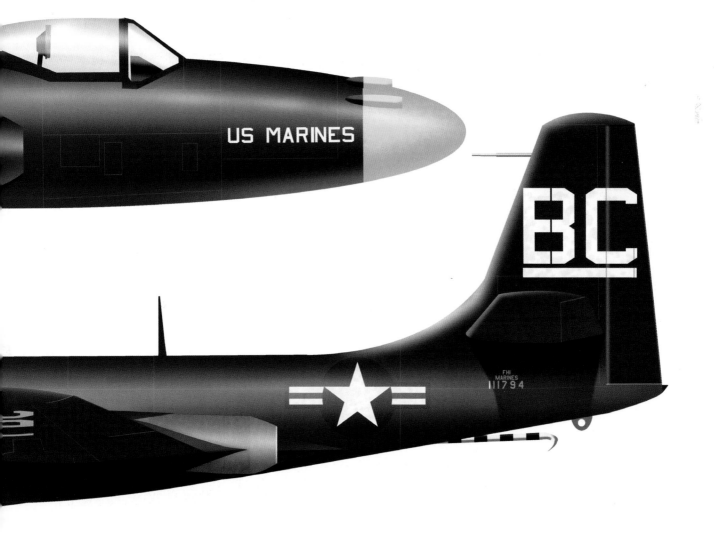

MCDONNELL F2H BANSHEE

McDonnell's underpowered Phantom was a fundamentally sound design – so when bigger engines became available the company simply scaled it up to accommodate them, producing the F2H Banshee.

F2H2
MARINES
123247

MARINES
VMF-224

LC

F2H2
MARINES
123228

MARINES
VMF-122

1948–1961

Even as the FH-1 Phantom was undergoing development during late 1944, McDonnell was preparing a larger but otherwise very similar design to take advantage of Westinghouse's new J34-WE-22 turbojet.

Where the Phantom's J30-WE-20 was 100in long with a diameter of 19in, the J34-WE-22 was 112in and 27in. McDonnell therefore scaled up the basic Phantom design to match. This was certainly worth doing because where the J30 produced a rather weedy 1600lb of thrust, the J34 promised a dramatic increase – 3000lb per engine.

On March 2, 1945, just five days before ordering 100 FH-1 Phantoms, the Navy gave McDonnell a contract for three prototypes of the scaled-up design under the designation XF2D-1. The extra power allowed the company to switch the four nose-mounted machine guns for four 20mm cannon in the same positions. The wings were larger than those of the Phantom but retained their ability to fold.

The valuable experience gained from building and flying the Phantom prototypes also fed into the new development programme and McDonnell was able to make numerous changes and improvements to the aircraft's

aerodynamic shape as well as to systems, access panels and other aspects of the design. It was named 'Banshee' by the company.

The company was already at the point of delivering the earliest FH-1s when the first prototype XF2H-1 flew on January 11, 1947. Following successful flight tests, the Navy ordered 56 production model F2H-1s on May 29, 1947.

The first of these were sent to the Naval Air Test Center and subsequently to Navy units VF-171 and VF-172. No Marine units operated the F2H-1. They would, however, make good use of the next variant. Even before the first F2H-1

▼ MCDONNELL F2H-2 BANSHEE

McDonnell F2H-2 Banshee, WK-7, VMF-224, MCAS Cherry Point, North Carolina, 1951. The Banshee was the first jet operated by VMF-224. Having previously operated F4U Corsairs, it flew the F2H for only one year before transitioning to the F9F Panther in 1952.

▼ MCDONNELL F2H-2 BANSHEE

McDonnell F2H-2 Banshee, LC-3, VMF-122, MCAS Beaufort, South Carolina, 1951. VMF-122 had been the first USMC squadron to operate jets with the FH-1 Phantom and also became the first to fly the new F2H Banshee in 1951.

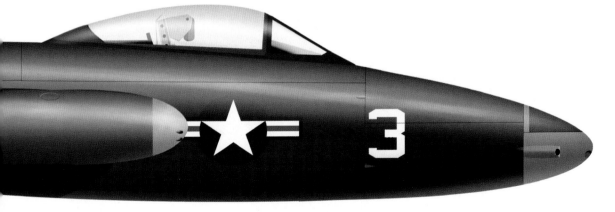

had been delivered, an order was placed for the significantly upgraded F2H-2.

This featured an ejection seat – a first for a McDonnell aircraft – wingtip tanks and four external hardpoints under each wing. Power was supplied by J34-WE-34s, producing 3250lb of thrust each, but this failed to translate into improved performance because the F2H-2 was 1300lb heavier than the F2H-1.

A further consequence of this extra weight was limited payload. The aircraft might have had eight positions for underwing stores but these could only accommodate up to 1540lb of conventional bombs or rockets in total. Also, the tip tanks could only be fuelled when the wings were in the down position. If the wings needed to be folded on a carrier deck, the tanks had to be drained first.

The F2H-2 would be the most-produced Banshee with 364 examples rolling off McDonnell's St Louis production line. Two Marine Corps squadrons flew it – VMF-122 and VMF-224 – with deliveries commencing in 1951. Both units were based at MCAS Cherry Point and both made a single deployment to the Mediterranean. In service,

▼ MCDONNELL F2H-2P BANSHEE

McDonnell F2H-2P Banshee, MW-1, VMJ-1, Pohang (K-3) Air Base, Korea, 1952.
VMJ-1 was the only USMC Banshee squadron to see combat during the Korean conflict; it operated the photo-reconnaissance variant, providing invaluable information on enemy positions.

the Banshee was known by the affectionate nickname 'Banjo'.

With F2H-2 production under way, the Navy decided it needed some fighters capable of carrying nuclear bombs. As a result, 27 F2H-2Bs were produced with strengthened port wings, reduced cannon armament, an inflight refuelling probe installed and a new bomb rack for carrying either a Mark 7 or Mark 8 bomb – but these were flown exclusively by the Navy, as were 14 F2H-2N night fighter variants fitted with AN/APS-19A radars in new plastic noses.

The USMC did, however, receive the reconnaissance version – the F2H-2P. This had a much longer nose than that of the standard F2H-2 and it was divided up into three sections with room to accommodate up to six high-resolution cameras in a variety of positions.

Both Marine Photo Reconnaissance Squadron One (VMJ-1) and VMJ-2 operated the F2H-2P – with VMJ-1's Banshees seeing combat in Korea. When it was established in late February 1952, VMJ-1 brought all Marine photo reconnaissance assets together in one

▼ MCDONNELL F2H-4 BANSHEE

McDonnell F2H-4 Banshee, LK-3, VMF-114, MCAS Cherry Point, North Carolina, 1953.
The F2H-4 was an improved variant of the Banshee with a new radar which gave all-weather capability.

place – five F2H-2P Banshees, four F7F-2P Tiger Cats, one F9F-2P Panther and one F4U-5P Corsair.

The unit was stationed at Pohang Airfield in Korea the following month and over time the Banshees became its mainstay. They were not as fast as the enemy's MiG-15s, however, which resulted in numerous engagements and near misses. Eventually, the USAF began providing F-86s to cover them but the

Marine pilots would later admit that they were unsure whether this was for their protection or because their unarmed Banshees made great bait to lure the enemy out.

By the end of the war in July 1953, VMJ-1 had shot more than 800,000ft of film in support of Marine ground forces and the Far East Air Force.

VMJ-2 would operate the type while stationed at MCAS Cherry Point, starting

in September 15, 1952, and its F2H-2Ps had mostly been replaced with F9F-6Ps by the end of 1955.

Meanwhile, McDonnell had been busy with another scaling exercise and had proposed a still larger version of the Banshee as a dedicated night and all-weather interceptor, replacing the F2H-2N. The new F2H-3 kept the engines of the F2H-2 but had a new fuselage that was 7ft longer, larger wings and a redesigned tail.

▼ MCDONNELL F2H-2 BANSHEE

McDonnell F2H-2 Banshee, 955, MCAS El Toro, California, 1958.
The F2H-2 Banshee had a rather short front line career and was soon transferred to reserve units – where it would remain well into the late 1950s.

Within the enlarged fuselage were a pair of new fuel tanks, making the wingtip tanks superfluous, and within the nose was an AN/APQ-41 radar. The first F2H-3 flew on March 29, 1952, and 250 were made – though none of them served with the Marines.

The last Banshee sub-type was the F2H-4 – another night and all-weather interceptor. It was based on the F2H-3 and externally looked identical. However, beneath the skin it had new J34-WE-38 engines offering 3600lb of thrust each and a new AN/APG-37 radar in its nose. The Navy ordered 150 F2H-4s and this time the Marine Corps received sufficient aircraft to equip three squadrons – VMF(AW)-114, VMF(AW)-214 'Black Sheep' and VMF(AW)-533 'Black Diamonds'

A total of 892 Banshees were built across the four variants. The type remained in front line service until 1959 and the last examples were retired from the Reserves in 1961. In September 1962 the F2H-3 was redesignated F-2C while the F2H-4 became the F-2D – though there were few if any aircraft left in service to receive these new codes.

▲ MCDONNELL F2H-4 BANSHEE

McDonnell F2H-4 Banshee, WE-14, VMF-214, MCAS Kaneohe Bay, Hawaii, 1957.
VMF-214, based on the Hawaiian islands, operated the Banshee from 1953 to 1958 before transitioning to the FJ-4 Fury.

NORTH AMERICAN FJ-2 AND FJ-3 FURY

North American's first generation FJ-1 Fury carrier fighter lacked performance when fully laden and was not adopted by the Marines. However, it set the scene for the USAF's F-86 Sabre, which itself was then navalised to produce a whole new Fury series.

1954-1962

The straight-winged FJ-1 Fury naval jet fighter was not a great success for North American but the company gained a lot of experience during its development. The requirement to make the aircraft suitable for carrier landings meant it had to be structurally stronger than a land-based fighter, with landing gear capable of absorbing heavy impacts.

In addition, before the FJ-1 was commissioned, North American had offered it with either swept or straight wings and the Navy had picked straight. With little known about the characteristics of swept wings at this time, it was feared that a swept wing fighter would be unable to land slowly – making it unsuitable for carrier operations.

When the USAAF issued a requirement for a new jet fighter in 1945, North American took the FJ-1 and removed all those aspects of its design which had been necessary for a naval fighter. The result was a much lighter aircraft with swept wings – the excellent F-86 Sabre.

The F-86 entered service with the USAF in 1949, two years after the beginning of the first Fury's brief career with the Navy, and quickly began building itself an enviable reputation. The Navy soon requested a navalised version, prompting North American to add carrier gear to the F-86E under project number NA-181. This included folding wings, an arrestor hook under the rear fuselage, a catapult bridle hook and a lengthened nosewheel leg.

NORTH AMERICAN FJ-2 FURY ▼

North American FJ-2 Fury, WR-5, VMF-312, MCAS Cherry Point, North Carolina, 1955.
VMF-312 acquired the FJ-2 Fury in 1954, operating the type for two years before the FJ-3 replaced it.

NORTH AMERICAN FJ-2 FURY ▼

North American FJ-2 Fury, MX-13, VMF-334, MCAS Miami, Florida, 1954.
The FJ-2 struggled through a brief operational career blighted by several shortcomings which were addressed by the new FJ-3 variant.

A letter contract for 300 examples was issued to North American on February 10, 1951, and three prototypes were ordered under the designation XFJ-2 on March 8, 1951. The first two were essentially standard F-86Es with carrier gear added because structural changes, such as the addition of folding wings, were not required at this stage. The third was a standard F-86E without carrier gear but with four 20mm cannon in its nose rather than the machine guns fitted to the USAF's F-86E.

The third of the three flew first – on December 27, 1951 – since the changes required were so slight. The first XFJ-2 with carrier gear began flight testing on February 14, 1952. Extensive experimentation during 1952 revealed that the FJ-2's undercarriage and arrestor hook were too weak for carrier landings and pilots found that its poor manoeuvrability on approach made the landing itself very difficult.

Design revisions were made and the production FJ-2 had a wheel track 8in wider than that of the original F-86E, folding wings, four 20mm cannon, a modified cockpit canopy for better visibility during deck landings, and substantially strengthened landing gear.

By now though, North American had already started work on a variant of the Fury which had the potential to be leaps and bounds ahead of the FJ-2 in performance terms. Project NA-194 involved swapping the FJ-2's J47-GE-2 engine for the Wright J65-W-2 – a licence-built version of the British Armstrong-Siddeley Sapphire turbojet. Where the J47 provided 6000lb of thrust, the J65 had a healthier 7800lb.

The Navy realised that this new variant offered a real advantage and ordered 289 of them on April 18, 1952 under the designation FJ-3.

Deliveries of the FJ-2 commenced in November 1952 but proceeded slowly since North American was busy building the F-86F for the Air Force. Just seven examples had been delivered by the time the Korean War ended – at which point the order for 300 FJ-2s was cut to 200.

The Navy was not particularly happy with the FJ-2s it received. Handling remained tricky when it came to carrier operations, the rudder apparently had a tendency to make an irritating buzzing noise at transonic speeds and worst of all the new F9F-6 Cougar had just become available – which, though slower, was much better suited to carrier operations.

As a result, FJ-2s were assigned almost exclusively to land-based Marine

NORTH AMERICAN FJ-2 FURY ▼

North American FJ-2 Fury, WU-6, VMF-235, MCAS El Toro, California, 1954.
Similarly to other USMC units, VMF-235 operated both the FJ-2 and FJ-3 Fury, transitioning from one to the other relatively quickly.

NORTH AMERICAN FJ-2 FURY ▼

North American FJ-2 Fury, AM-1, VMF-451, NAF Atsugi, Japan, 1954.
VMF-451 received the FJ-2 in 1954 before deployment to Naval Air Facility Atsugi in Japan.

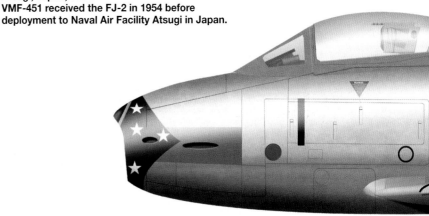

NORTH AMERICAN FJ-3 FURY ▼

North American FJ-3 Fury, LC-2, VMF-122, MCAS Cherry Point, North Carolina, 1956.
As with other aircraft operated by the USMC, the FJ-3 was first delivered to VMF-122.

Corps units. Meanwhile, the fifth FJ-2 off the production line was modified to accommodate a J65-W-2 engine and made its first flight in this configuration on July 3, 1953. Flight testing revealed that further power gains could be made by enlarging the FJ-2 nose intake so this change was carried forward to the production model.

The first FJ-3 was flown on December 11, 1953, with the improved J65-W-4 engine. Early FJ-3s had wing slats but these were later deleted and extended wing leading edges were fitted instead, with a leading edge fence. As a result, wing area was increased from 287.9sq ft to 302.3sq ft and the extra space within the wing allowed the FJ-3 to carry another 124 gallons of fuel. Many of the early FJ-3s would later be retrofitted with the new wing leading edge.

By now it was clear that the FJ-2 was going to be little more than an interim type but deliveries to the Marines commenced as planned nevertheless. The first operational unit to receive it was VMF-122 at Cherry Point in January 1954. Eventually the type would equip at least seven units including VMF-122, VMF-224, VMF-232, VMF-235, VMF-312, VMF-334 and VMF-451.

Twenty-four FJ-3s had been delivered to the Navy by July 1954 and testing revealed few problems. While VF-173 was first to receive the FJ-3 in September 1954 and the Navy would receive the majority of the FJ-3s manufactured, the type was operated by at least four Marines squadrons – VMF-122, VMF-251, VMF-313 and VMF-333 – with a fifth, VMF-235, operating the FJ-3M.

This latter variant was introduced in 1956. As more Furies were produced, a change was made on the assembly line to incorporate two hardpoints beneath each wing. While the stations closest to the fuselage could only handle rocket pods or 500lb bombs, the outer stations could be used to carry either 1000lb bombs or AIM-9A Sidewinder launch rails. About 80 Furies were built with the latter and given the designation FJ-3M.

Production of the FJ-3 ended in August 1956 after a total of 538 had been made. The last 149 were fitted with the J65-W-4D engine, which had 7660lb of thrust. The last FJ-3s were phased out of Reserve units in 1962, this last handful being redesignated F-1C under the new Tri-Service designation scheme on October 1, 1962.

NORTH AMERICAN FJ-3 FURY ▽

North American FJ-3 Fury, DN-3, VMF-333, MCAS Beaufort, South Carolina, 1958.
VMF-333 received its first jet aircraft (FJ-3s) in 1957, having previously operated A-1 Skyraiders.

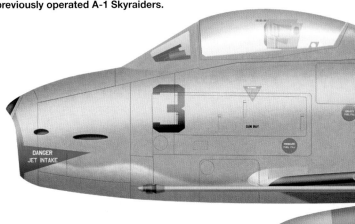

NORTH AMERICAN FJ-3 FURY ▽

North-American FJ-3 Fury, DW-611, VMF-251, MCAS Miami, Florida, 1957.
The FJ-3 differed significantly form the previous FJ-2, having a new engine and systems plus aerodynamic modifications. VMF-251 operated the FJ-3 for about a year before being reequipped with FJ-4s.

NORTH AMERICAN FJ-3 FURY ▽

North American FJ-3 Fury, 7Z-13, MAR South Weymouth, Mariland, 1960.
The last USMC units to operate the FJ-3 were from the Marine Air Reserve.

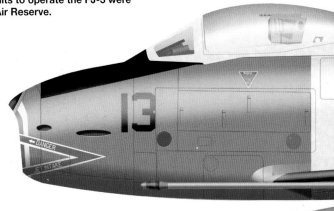

MARINES
VMF-333
FJ3
136022
DN

MARINES
VMF-251
FJ-3
135935
DW

MARINES
SO. WEYMOUTH
FJ-3
136037
13
7Z
6037

NORTH AMERICAN FJ-4 FURY

The final Fury was the ultimate development of the sprawling F-86 Sabre lineage – so heavily upgraded that it only superficially resembled the original aircraft.

NORTH AMERICAN FJ-4 FURY ▼

North American FJ-4 Fury, AM-1, VMF-451, NAS Atsugi, Japan, 1956.
The FJ-4 Fury entered USMC service with VMF-451.

1955–CIRCA 1966

NORTH AMERICAN FJ-4 FURY ▼

North American FJ-4 Fury, WT-3, VMF-232, MCAS Kaneohe Bay, Hawaii, 1958.
VMF-232 operated the FJ-4 Fury in the Pacific, being deployed during the second Taiwan strait crisis in 1958.

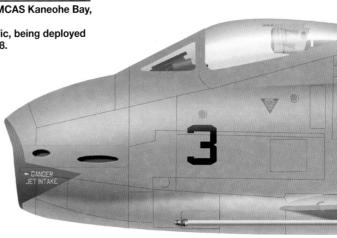

While the FJ-2 was basically an F-86 with naval gear tacked on and the FJ-3 was mostly an FJ-2 with a better engine, the Navy had already set its sights on a true evolutionary leap for the Fury by June 1953. The prototype FJ-3 had not even taken its first flight when the Navy asked North American to create a new version able to hit Mach 0.95 without an afterburner and combat capable up to 49,000ft.

This was a tall order given that the aircraft's basic design had originally been set out during the Second World War but the company rose to the challenge with project NA-208. Rather than being a modification of the existing Sabre/Fury airframe, a whole new fuselage would be created with an additional fuel tank added below the engine, a full length dorsal spine, new nose intake and new cockpit.

The wings too would be completely new – thinner and longer with a 2ft greater span and a surface area increase

to 338.66sq ft. They featured a new drooping leading edge to improve low speed handling and to provide extra lift during landing, a four-degree washout at the wingtip and trailing edge ailerons at mid-span. They folded further outboard than those of the earlier Furies as well and part way through the production run an inflight refuelling probe was added as standard beneath the port wing.

The uprated F-86 landing gear which had caused problems during the early stages of the Fury's career was completely disposed of and replaced with a bespoke design which increased the mainwheel track from 9ft to 11ft 7in.

Armament remained four nose-mounted 20mm cannon but ammunition capacity was reduced to 576 rounds from the FJ-3's 648 rounds, with only 500 usually being carried. The space freed up by limiting ammo was then used to provide extra armour. Each wing could be fitted with two pylons – for a total of four – with the inboard stations able to carry drop tanks or stores up to 2000lb

each and the outboard stations able to manage up to 500lb. The total possible load was 3000lb. A single AIM-9A Sidewinder could be carried on any of the four stations and bombs or rocket pods could also be fitted, though the FJ-4 was primarily intended for air-to-air combat.

The first of two FJ-4 prototypes (the XFJ-4 designation was never used) made its flight debut on October 28, 1954, with North American test pilot Richard 'Dick' Wenzell at the controls. This example was fitted with a Wright J65-W-4 engine – the same powerplant

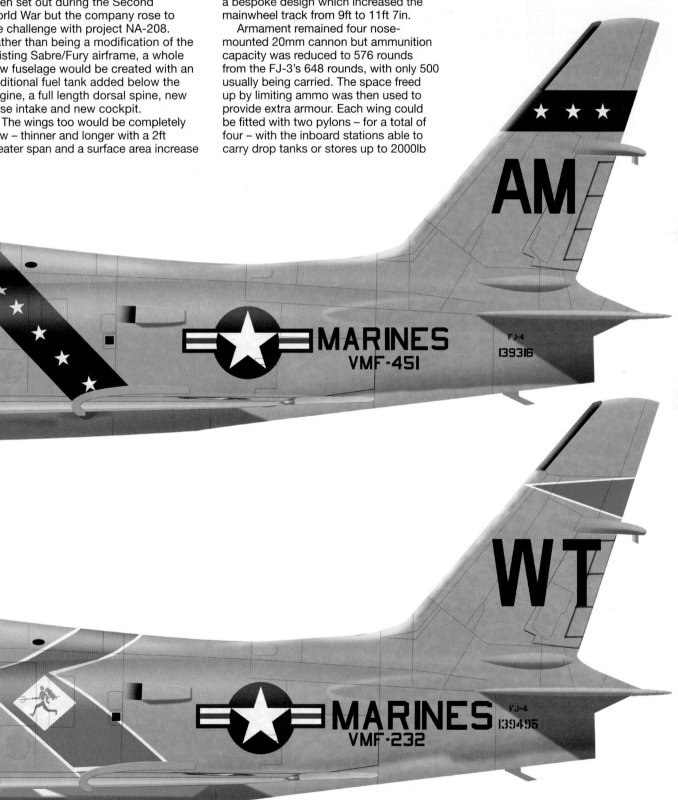

▼ NORTH AMERICAN FJ-4B FURY

North American FJ-4B Fury, WP-6, VMA-223, MCAS Cherry Point, North Carolina, 1959.
The FJ-4B was an improved variant with added air-to-ground capability. VMA-223 operated the Fury for about four years before being re-equipped with A-4 Skyhawks.

NORTH AMERICAN FJ-4 FURY ▼

North American FJ-4 Fury, WU-6, VMF-235, MCAS Beaufort, South Carolina, 1957.
VMF-235 was based at MCAS El Toro, California, before being relocated to the other side of the country – to MCAS Beaufort, South Carolina – in 1957.

used by the FJ-3. The first production FJ-4s, powered by the J65-W-16A, were completed in February 1955. The new engine provided 7700lb of thrust but the FJ-4's performance was no better than that of the FJ-3 due to weight increases.

As had been the case with the FJ-3, production was slow with only 17 FJ-4s being built during the remainder of 1955. A further 113 followed in 1956 and nearly all FJ-4s went to the USMC; the first unit to receive it was VMF-451, followed by VMF-232, VMF-235, VMF-334 and more.

A handful were delivered to the Navy and served with the Replacement Air Group, VA-126 at NAS Miramar. After the initial batch of 150 FJ-4s had been delivered, production switched to a new variant – the FJ-4B.

Prior to the commencement of FJ-4B production however, a pair of standard FJ-4s were retrofitted with AR-1 rocket motors in their rear fuselages under the designation FJ-4F. These motors, produced by Rocketdyne, a division of North American, were to be tested in

support of Chance Vought's XF8U-3 Crusader III programme. The Crusader III, a competitor for the F-4 Phantom II, would have been a mixed propulsion fighter with a rocket motor providing 8000lb of thrust to supplement its single Pratt & Whitney J75-P-5A turbojet. The original plan called for six FJ-4Fs but only two had been converted by the time the Crusader III programme was cancelled.

The FJ-4B, intended to be the ground-attack version, was the last variant of the FJ-4 and the last iteration of the

▼ NORTH AMERICAN FJ-4 FURY

North American FJ-4 Fury, WS-4, VMF-323, MCAS Miramar, California, 1957.
Originally designated VMF-323 'Death Rattlers', the squadron became VMA-323 in June 1952 – only to become VMF-323 again shortly after receiving its first FJ-4s. Seven years later, in 1964, it would become VMFA-323.

NORTH AMERICAN FJ-4B FURY ▽

North American FJ-4B Fury, WE-13, VMA-214, MCAS Yuma,
Arizona, 1962.
VMA-214 operated the FJ-4B Fury for about three years before being
equipped with A-4 Skyhawks. FJ-4s could carry external fuel tanks in
addition to the fixed refuelling probe, increasing operational range.

▼ NORTH AMERICAN FJ-4B FURY

**North American FJ-4B Fury, WD-7, VMA-212, USS *Oriskany*
(CVA-34), 1960.**
VMA-212 operated the Fury for about two years, both from land
bases and aboard aircraft carriers. This aircraft is armed with
AIM-9 Sidewinders.

▼ NORTH AMERICAN FJ-4B FURY

North American FJ-4 Fury, WV-9, VMF-334, NAS Atsugi, Japan, 1957.
VMF-334 was one of several USMC squadrons to operate the Fury
from Japan.

F-86 lineage overall. Its wings were strengthened so it could manage up to six pylons – three under each wing – carrying a total of 6000lb in stores. Any of these stations could accommodate rocket pods or ASM-N-7 (redesignated AGM-12 in 1962) Bullpup air-to-surface missiles. If Bullpups were carried, the inner station on the right hand wing would be used for a Bullpup guidance transmitter pod. The mid-wing stations could carry drop tanks up to 200 gallons and the outboard stations could carry tanks up to 150 gallons.

Another option was to carry a single Mark 7 nuclear bomb on the left centre pylon. In this configuration it was standard practice to also carry three drop tanks. The nuclear mission would also involve a buddy refuelling system to further extend the bomber's range. Two FJ-4Bs would take off, one carrying the weapon and the other carrying only drop tanks. At a pre-determined refuelling point, the bomber would refuel from the 'buddy' before continuing on to its target – while the 'buddy' tanker turned around and returned to base.

When an FJ-4B was called upon to carry a nuclear weapon, it was fitted with the Low Altitude Bombing System (LABS) computer which allowed the pilot to 'toss' the bomb and begin flying away before it detonated. Installation of LABS involved removal of the FJ-4's usual radar ranging gunsight.

In order to improve low-altitude, high-Mach handling the FJ-4B also had spoilers added ahead of the trailing edge flaps. Extra air brakes were also added on the sides of the fuselage aft of the wing trailing edge to reduce landing speed for carrier operations. With the brakes deployed, the pilot could approach with the engine set at a higher RPM than would otherwise have been possible – avoiding rough engine running and providing increased potential for a go-around if needed. Assuming the landing proceeded smoothly, the air brakes would close automatically when the undercarriage was lowered to prevent them from scraping on the carrier deck.

The first FJ-4B flew on December 4, 1956, and full scale production commenced during 1957. By May of 1958, when the last one was delivered, a total of 222 had been made.

Marine attack squadrons VMA-212, VMA-214 and VMA-223 were all equipped with the FJ-4B – though the type was destined to serve for only four years before being relegated to reserve units where it would remain, with its nuclear capability deleted, for a handful of additional years.

When the US Defense Department implemented its tri-service designation system in 1962, the FJ-4 became the F-1E and the FJ-4B became the AF-1E – though it matter little since they had all been withdrawn from active service by that point.

GRUMMAN F9F PANTHER

The Panther was the exactly what the Marine Corps needed exactly when it needed it. Able to perform both CAS and anti-air missions, it would serve as the USMC's primary fighter during the Korean War.

GRUMMAN F9F-2 PANTHER ▷

Grumman F9F-2 Panther, WL-2, VMF-311, Pohang Air Base (K-3), Korea, 1952.
VMF-311 flew the F9F Panther in combat in Korea, being the first land based USMC jet squadron to operate in that conflict. Among the unit's pilots at this time was future astronaut and United States Senator John Glenn.

1949–1958

GRUMMAN F9F-2 PANTHER ▷

Grumman F9F-2 Panther, WT-5, VMF-232, MCAS El Toro, California, 1953.
The Panther was VMF-232's first jet but it would transition to the Fury within a year.

F9F-2
MARINES
123507

MARINES
VMF-232

When Grumman first started work on the F9F it was to be a two-seater four-engined night fighter competitor for Douglas's F3D Skyknight. A prototype was planned under the designation XF9F-1 but the Skyknight was declared the winner on October 9, 1946, and the XF9F-1 was cancelled before it could be built. It may not have seemed it at the time but this was perhaps the best thing that could have happened to the F9F.

Grumman returned to the drawing board and split the basic layout, Design G-79, into four different lines of development. One of these had a turbojet in each of its wings, two of them had a mixture of both rockets and turbojets, and the final design had just a single turbojet. It was this layout, Study D, which seemed the most promising to the Navy when Grumman put forward its proposals.

An order was placed for a trio of prototypes. Two of these would be powered by the 5000lb thrust Taylor Turbine Corporation J42-TT-2 – a licence-built version of the Rolls-Royce Nene – under the designation XF9F-2. However, the corporation was new to turbojet manufacturing and struggled to get started. As a result, it was forced to import six Nenes from Britain and hand them straight over to Grumman.

The third prototype, designated XF9F-3, would be powered by Allison's 4600lb thrust J33-A-8, which the Navy considered less risky than relying on Taylor and its British-designed engine – even though the J33 was less powerful.

Fitted with its British engines, the first XF9F-2 made its aerial debut on November 24, 1947, flown by test pilot Corwin H 'Corky' Meyer, and the second XF9F-2 took to the air just five days later. Neither had any weapons installed nor even an ejection seat. Testing proceeded quickly and it was discovered that the aircraft suffered from longitudinal instability at all speeds and snaking was also an issue. The snaking was cured by enlarging the fin and rudder while adding baffles to the fuel tanks addressed the instability. The rear fuselage was also strengthened.

Taylor was later persuaded to relinquish the Nene manufacturing licence and it was bought by the much more experienced Pratt & Whitney. The sole XF9F-3 eventually flew on August 16, 1948, and even though it found that the J33 was neither as reliable nor as powerful as hoped, a full production series of F9F-3s was ordered alongside the first run of F9F-2s.

Grumman had given most of its fighters up to this point a feline name – F4F Wildcat, F6F Hellcat, F7F Tigercat and F8F Bearcat – so 'Panther' was chosen for the F9F.

The production F9F-2, with its centrally mounted engine, was of all-metal construction and its mid-mounted straight wings had flaps on both leading and trailing edges. They folded hydraulically, just outboard of the main

WL

F9F-2
MARINES
127207

MARINES
VMF-311

5

GRUMMAN F9F-2 PANTHER ▼

Grumman F9F-2 Panther, AE-6, VMF-115, Pohang Air Base (K-3), Korea, 1952.
VMF-115 was the first Marine squadron to operate Panthers, receiving the first one in 1949. Deployed to Korea in 1952, the squadron was heavily involved in combat and would expend more ordnance in-theatre than any other Marine jet fighter unit.

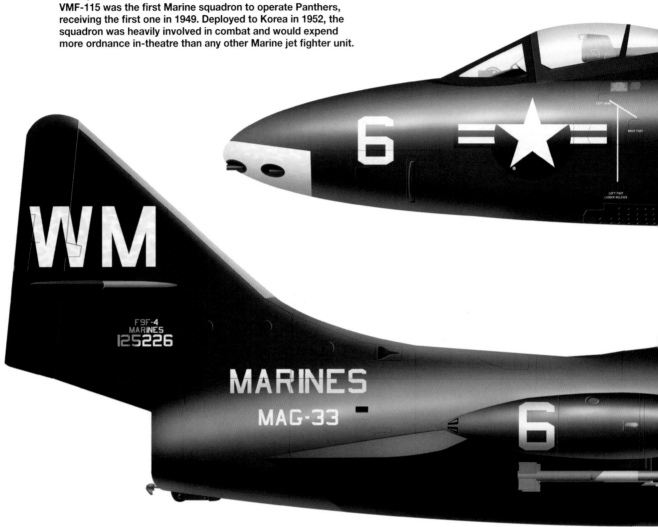

GRUMMAN F9F-4 PANTHER ▼

Grumman F9F-4 Panther, WR-13, VMF-312, MCAS Miami, Florida, 1954.
After operating F4U Corsairs in Korea, VMF-312 returned to the USA to begin the transitioning to F9F Panthers in 1953.

▼ GRUMMAN F9F-4 PANTHER

Grumman F9F-4 Panther, WM-6, MAG-33, Pohang Air Base (K-3), Korea, 1952.
Marine Air Group 33 was originally established during the Second World War. Another Marine unit deployed to Korea, its first offensive mission there would be an eight-plane strike package against the North Korean 6th Division in the Jinju area.

undercarriage wheels, but could not quite reach a vertical position – sticking out slightly on each side instead. Wingtip tanks were added from the 13th example off the production line and this took total fuel capacity up to 923 gallons. There were initially three hardpoints beneath each wing which could be used for bombs or rocket launchers.

The undercarriage was the by-now-standard tricycle arrangement with the nosewheel retracting rearwards and the main wheels retracting towards the fuselage. Behind the nosewheel well was a split perforated air brake and a 'stringer' type arresting hook was installed just below the jet exhaust.

The aircraft's straight tailplanes were high up on the tail fin and the turbojet exhausted below it. While the type's main engine intakes were in its wingroots, a pair of auxiliary intake doors were built into the aircraft's back to provide an emergency alternative if additional airflow was needed. The tail could be removed as a single piece so that the engine could be accessed for maintenance or replacement.

Inside the pressurised cockpit were a Martin-Baker ejection seat and a Mark 8 computing optical gunsight for the pilot. The full-vision canopy slid rearwards to provide access and a small retractable step was built into the lower fuselage to

help the pilot clamber up. At the front of the aircraft, the nosecone could be slid forwards to provide access to the four 20mm M3 cannon in the lower section and their 760 rounds of ammunition (190 per gun).

The first F9F-2 flew in August 1949 and while trials were conducted using what was now the J42-P-4 engine, this would be replaced by the J42-P-6 and then the J42-P-8 with a different ignition system. All versions of the J42 still offered 5000lb thrust or 5750lb with water injection.

Only a handful of F9F-3s were built before it was concluded that the J33's problems could not easily be remedied

GRUMMAN F9F-5 PANTHER ▲

Grumman F9F-5 Panther, WP-24, VMA-223, MCAS El Toro, California, 1956.
F9F Panthers were the first jet aircraft to equip VMA-223 – in 1950. This aircraft is seen years later sporting the new light gull grey-white colour scheme.

and all production was switched to the F9F-2. The F9F-3s were retrofitted with the J42 and became impossible, visually, to distinguish from those aircraft built as F9F-2s, of which 564 were built.

Many early F9F-2s were modified to accept an additional hardpoint under each wing, making them F9F-2Bs. The inboard pylon could carry a 150 gallon drop tank or a 1000lb bomb and the outer three could each take either a 250lb bomb or a set of 5in HVAR rockets. Total load was up to a maximum of 2000lb. Eventually, all F9F-2s were brought up to F9F-2B standard and the 'B' was dropped.

The first Marine Corps squadron equipped with the F9F-2 Panther was VMF-115 in 1949. This same unit was the first, on November 20, 1950, to carrier qualify all 18 of its pilots – aboard

USS Franklin D. Roosevelt. Less than three weeks later, on December 7, 1950, Panther-equipped VMF-311 was the first land-based Marine jet squadron to provide close air support for Marines in Korea.

During the early stages of the war, before the F2H-2P Banshee became available, there was an urgent need for photo reconnaissance and a small number of F9F-2s were fitted with a new nose housing vertical and side-looking cameras as F9F-2Ps.

F9F-4 AND F9F-5
Even as the first F9F-2s were being delivered in 1949, two further variants of the Panther were being ordered from Grumman – the F9F-4 and F9F-5. The former was to be equipped with the

GRUMMAN F9F-5 PANTHER ▼

Grumman F9F-5 Panther, WK-11, VMA-224, MCAS El Toro, California, 1956.
VMA-224 operated the Panther for around four years before being re-equipped with A-4 Skyhawks in 1956.

GRUMMAN F9F-5 PANTHER ▽

Grumman F9F-5 Panther, WS-5, VMA-323, MCAS El Toro, California, 1956.
The Death Rattlers, VMA-323, flew the F4U Corsair in Korea before
converting to Panthers in 1953.

GRUMMAN F9F-2B PANTHER ▽

Grumman F9F-2B, WL-2, VMF-311, Pohang Air Base (K-3), Korea, 1952.
Marine Panthers were worked hard in Korea, as can be seen by the
numerous missions marking displayed on this VMF-311 'Tomcats' aircraft.

▼ GRUMMAN F9F-5 PANTHER

Grumman F9F-5 Panther, LC-221, VMF-122, USS *Coral Sea* (CV-43), 1953. VMF-122 – known as the Candystripers at this point – embarked on a six month cruise aboard USS *Coral Sea* in the Mediterranean during February 1953. Their 20 Panthers flew 2700 hours on 1800 missions, making more than 1750 deck landings without a single loss.

Allison J33-A-16 (an uprated version of the J33-A-8 which had powered the F9F-3), providing 6950lb of thrust with water injection, while the latter would have the Pratt & Whitney J48-P-6 – which was another licence-built British design, this time the Rolls-Royce Tay – with 7250lb of thrust with water/alcohol injection.

Aside from their engines, the F9F-4 and F9F-5 differed from the F9F-2 and F9F-3 in being 19.5in longer to improve overall fuel capacity from 923 to 1003 gallons. Their tail fins were also increased in both height and surface area to further improve stability and the engine intakes were redesigned. The extra power meant that a greater weight of underwing stores could be carried to – up to 3465lb on the F9F-5.

The two types were developed in parallel, just as the F9F-2 and F9F-3 had been, and the outcome was largely similar. Once again, the J33 was underpowered in comparison to its rival and proved to be unreliable. The first F9F-5 made its flight debut on December 21, 1949, with the first F9F-4 following on July 6, 1950. Deliveries of the F9F-5 commenced just four months later. A total of 109 F9F-4s were manufactured compared to 616 F9F-5s – making the latter the most common Panther overall.

Thirty-six F9F-5s were modified to became F9F-5P photo recon variants. These differed from the earlier F9F-2P in having noses that were 12in longer so larger cameras and their associated equipment could be fitted. These aircraft were further altered so that no external stores could be carried except for 150 gallon external tanks on the inboard underwing pylon. They were also fitted with a General Electric G-3 autopilot unit.

The Marine Corps operated F9F-2Bs, F9F-4s and F9F-5s exclusively in the ground-attack role during the Korean War. These Panthers equipped numerous units, including VMF-115, VMF-122, VMF-211, VMF-213, VMF-214, VMF-233, VMF-224, VMF-232, VMF-234, VMF-235, VMF-311, VMF-312, VMF-314, VMF-324, VMF-334 and VMF-451. Reconnaissance squadrons VMJ-1 and VMJ-3 flew the F9F-5P.

Panthers provided invaluable air support during many of the fiercest battles of the war, including Bunker Hill, the Battles of the Hook, the Battle for Outpost Vegas and the Battle of Chosin Reservoir. Most Panthers had been phased out of active service by 1956 but two Marine reserve squadrons, VMF-213 and VMF-214, both based at Minneapolis, continued to operate them until 1958.

When the new aircraft designation system was introduced in 1962, even though the type had long been retired from front line service, the F9F-4 became the F-9C, the F9F-5 the F-9D and the F9F-5P the RF-9D.

GRUMMAN F9F COUGAR

Arriving too late to see combat in Korea, Grumman's swept-wing Panther – renamed Cougar – saw limited but notable service with the Marines.

1952-1974

When the straight-winged Panther encountered the swept-wing MiG-15 over the battlefields of Korea in 1950, it became clear that for all its otherwise outstanding qualities Grumman's design was lacking aerodynamically. Both aircraft were powered by a derivative of the Rolls-Royce Nene turbojet yet the Russian design was almost 100mph faster.

From the outset, Grumman had taken a conservative line with the F9F and the result was a usable and reliable aircraft. Vought, Douglas and McDonnell, in contrast, continued to struggle with their advanced swept-wing Cutlass, Skyray and Demon designs respectively. But with the Korea War raging and the Panther fighting for survival against swept-winged opponents, it was clear to both the Navy and Grumman that urgent action was needed.

The result was project G-93 which, at first glance, looked a lot like a standard F9F-5 but with 35-degree sweptback wings and new swept tailplanes. There were a range of further subtle changes however – the fuselage was stretched by 2ft, allowing a larger forward internal fuel tank to be fitted, the wingroot intakes were extended further forwards and the wing root fillets were made larger. Wingtip fuel tanks were deleted from the design and the new wings, which had a greater surface area (300sq ft) than those of the original Panther (250sq ft), had fuel tanks installed in the leading edge.

In addition, the new wings had large trailing edge flaps for increased low speed lift along with long leading edge slats. Flaperons replaced ailerons on top of each wing to control rolling movement.

The company was given a contract to modify three existing F9F-5s as prototypes for the design on March 2, 1951. Rather than allocate a new designation however, the Navy decided to keep the design within the F9F series. This was probably for budgetary reasons, since it was easier to request funding for an improved version of an existing design than for a completely new and untested one. However, Grumman was allowed to give the aircraft a new name and chose 'Cougar'.

The three prototypes, based on F9F-5 airframes from the assembly line that had not yet been completed, were given the designation XF9F-6. Since the other modifications to the basic design were relatively straightforward, work on the first three Cougars – two flying examples and one static airframe for testing – went ahead very quickly and test pilot Fred C Rowley flew the first one on September 20, 1951.

It soon became obvious that the Panther had indeed been severely handicapped by its straight wings. The Cougar prototypes could fly up to 50mph faster while low speed handling, which had been the greatest concern when it came to fitting naval types with swept wings, proved to be acceptable. Like the Panther, the Cougar had four 20mm cannon, but unlike the Panther the F9F-6 only had two underwing hardpoints.

▼ **GRUMMAN F9F-6 COUGAR**

Grumman F9F-6 Cougar, SA-128, VMFT-10, MCAS El Toro, California, 1957.
The F9F Cougar was a design evolution of the F9F Panther and featured many new characteristics – the most visible of which was the new swept wing.

▼ **GRUMMAN F9F-8 COUGAR**

Grumman F9F-8 Cougar, ED-13, VMA-533, MCAS Cherry Point, North Carolina, 1958.
F9F-8s could be equipped with a fixed nose-mounted in-flight refuelling probe.

These were typically used for drop tanks but they could be made to accommodate stores up to 1000lb each.

Flight testing also indicated a serious problem. When the aircraft reached transonic speeds, control reversal could occur – potentially resulting in the loss of both aircraft and pilot. This was not an unfamiliar problem however, since North American and the USAF had already encountered it with the F-86, the root cause being identified as the tailplanes.

As originally designed, the Cougar's horizontal tail surfaces were fixed with moving elevators to the rear for pitch control. Experience with the F-86 had shown that swapping this arrangement

for all-moving tailplanes – where the whole surface could be controlled hydraulically – cured the control reversibility issue. Grumman test pilot Corwin 'Corky' Meyer was dispatched to Edwards Air Force Base in California to test an F-86E fitted with the 'flying tail' and found that it did indeed work as advertised, allowing normal flight at transonic speeds.

Meyer recommended that the 'flying tail' be adopted for the Cougar and Grumman agreed to make the change.

Aside from control reversal, the Cougar was also found to suffer from somewhat ineffective lateral and longitudinal control. Consequently large

17

VK

138855

MARINES
VMA-121

MT

F9F-6P
128310

MARINES

wing fences were added to reduce airflow down the span of the wing and funnel it towards the control surfaces.

While the first 30 Cougars off the production line were fitted with the J48-P-6A, with 7000lb of thrust, the rest had the J48-P-8 with an output of 7250lb. An impressive 646 F9F-6s were built but nearly all of them went to US Navy units with the type only being flown by the Marines when it was allocated to reserve units.

However, towards the end of F9F-6's production run, a total of 60 were fitted with the same camera nose as the reconnaissance Panther under the designation F9F-6P. These aircraft were divided between two Navy composite units and Marine squadron VMJ-2. The latter would then be merged with VMC-2 on December 1, 1955, to form VMCJ-2.

Where the F9F-3 was the Allison-engined counterpart of the Pratt & Whitney-engined F9F-2, and the F9F-4 was the Allison-engined counterpart of the F9F-5, there was also an Allison-engined counterpart to the F9F-6 – unsurprisingly designated F9F-7. Even less surprising was that for the third time Allison's engine played second fiddle to the superior licence-made P&W unit.

Just 168 F9F-7s were made, fitted with the J33-A-16A, and the first of them flew in March 1953. The production run continued until June 1954, with some F9F-7s being delivered directly to the reserves, so unwanted were they by the front line units. As had happened twice before, most were later retrofitted with a J48 variant to become pseudo F9F-6s. No F9F-7s served with the Marines.

The F9F-6, and to a lesser extent the F9F-7, had proven the benefits of swept wings to both Grumman and the Navy but during testing it occurred to the company's engineers that the wing design could be taken even further. A new wing was created which had enlarged outer panels, increasing low speed handling performance, and an increased chord outboard of the wing fence. The leading edge slats were deleted from the design and a larger fillet was added at the wing trailing edge, going all the way to the end of the fuselage. Each wing had an additional pylon added, allowing rocket pods, bombs up to 500lb or Sidewinder missiles to be carried.

At the same time, Grumman took the opportunity to get the best out of the fuselage as well. A new engine was available, the J48-P-8A, which offered

▼ **GRUMMAN F9F-8B COUGAR**

Grumman F9F-8B Cougar, VK-17, VMA-121, MCAS El Toro, California, 1958.
F9F-8B had a more robust air-to-ground capability, being equipped with the Low Altitude Bombing System (LABS).

▼ **GRUMMAN F9F-6P COUGAR**

Grumman F9F-6P Cougar, MT-11, VMJ-1, MCAS Cherry Point, North Carolina, 1956.
VMJ-1, Marine Photographic Squadron One, flew Banshees in Korea before being re-equipped with Cougars and later merged with Marine Composite Squadron One, VMC-1, to become VMCJ-1 in 1958.

GRUMMAN F9F-8T COUGAR ▼

Grumman F9F-8T Cougar, SD-17, VMT-2, MCAS El Toro, California, 1959.
The two-seat F9F-8T variant was used by several training squadrons of the USMC; it would be redesignated TF-9J after the implementation of the1962 United States Tri-Service aircraft designation system.

CM

F9F-6P
134446

MARINES

TN

F9F-8P
144382

MARINES
VMCJ-3

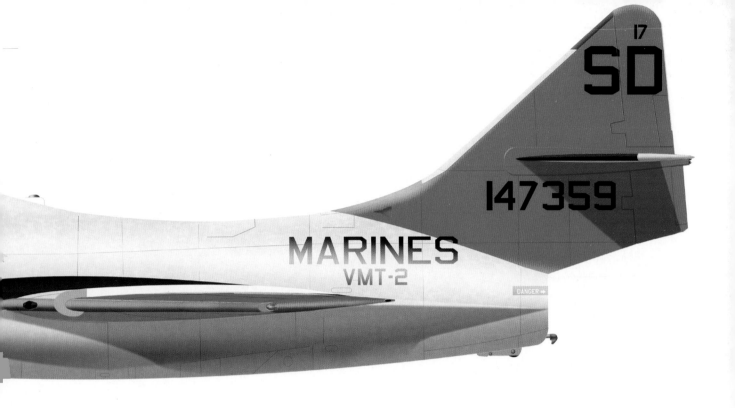

▼ GRUMMAN F9F-6P COUGAR

Grumman F9F-6P Cougar, CM-09, VMJ-2, MCAS
Cherry Point, North Carolina, 1956.
The F9F-6P was a Cougar modified for photographic
reconnaissance with several cameras in its nose.

▼ GRUMMAN F9F-8P COUGAR

Grumman F9F-8P Cougar, TN-2, VMCJ-3, MCAS El
Toro, California, 1957.
The final reconnaissance version of the Cougar,
the F9F-8P featured an elongated nose to allow the
installation of additional cameras.

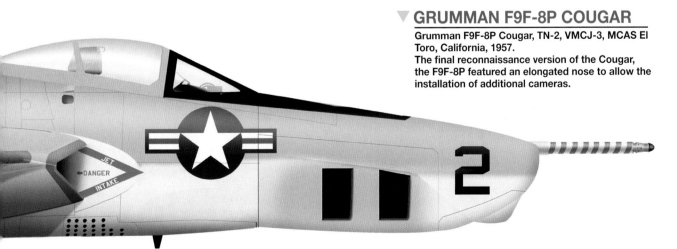

GRUMMAN TF-9J COUGAR ▼

Grumman TF-9J Cougar, TM-4, H&MS-11, MCAS El Toro, California, 1967.
The squadron saw service in Vietnam using TF-9Js in the FAC role. The crews found they were hampered by the aircraft's limited endurance, lack of agility and poor communication capabilities.

8500lb of thrust with water injection but rather than boosting performance this extra output was swallowed up by weight increases overall. In particular, the fuselage was stretched by 8in to create even more space for the internal fuel tanks, increasing capacity by 140 gallons.

This new variant was designated F9F-8 and the first example made its flight debut on December 18, 1953. Production commenced shortly thereafter and deliveries began on February 29, 1954. It would continue until March 22, 1957, with 601 having been built. This time, finally, there would be no Allison-engined second-stringer.

One variant of the F9F-8 was the F9F-8B, fitted with LABS and capable

of carrying tactical nuclear weapons. Another was the unarmed F9F-8P reconnaissance platform. This had a longer nose than that of the earlier F9F-5P and F9F-6P – stretching the aircraft's original 42ft 2in length to 44ft 9in. This flat-sided, noticeably drooping snout had a total of seven ports for forward-facing, vertical and oblique cameras. It also housed the necessary equipment for inflight refuelling.

The first F9F-8P flew on February 18, 1955, and 110 were produced.

Work on the F9F-8T trainer variant began in November 1953 as project G-105, a private venture since the Navy had not identified a need for the type. When it became aware of Grumman's

two-seater though, the Navy did authorise the modification of a single existing airframe to create a prototype, designated YF9F-8T. The fuselage was lengthened 34in to allow room for the second cockpit, making this the second longest Cougar at 44ft 4$\frac{1}{4}$in. The extra length was still not quite enough, however, so the rear cockpit also ate into the aircraft's fuel tank, reducing fuel capacity from 847 to 730 gallons. In addition, two of the Cougar's four cannon were removed. The trainer prototype flew for the first time on April 4, 1956.

When the development programme for Navy's chosen trainer, the Lockheed T2V-1 SeaStar, hit difficulties, the two-seat Cougar was re-evaluated and an order

GRUMMAN TF-9J COUGAR ▼

Grumman TF-9J Cougar, YU-2, H&MS-13, Chu Lai,
Vietnam, 1967.
Four TF-9Js of H&MS-13 (Headquarters and
Maintenance Squadron 13) were used in the
Forward Air Controller (FAC) role to direct airstrikes
against enemy positions during 1966-67.

▼ GRUMMAN F9F-8B COUGAR

Grumman F9F-8B Cougar, WL-5, VMA-311, MCAS El Toro, 1958.
The F9F-8B could carry nuclear weaponry. This one is depicted
carrying a Mark 12 nuclear bomb.

was placed for 399 production examples
under the designation F9F-8T.

Unlike the F9F-6, which was really
intended for air-to-air combat and
therefore less than ideal for Marine Corps
service, the F9F-8 was a somewhat
better fit – with its additional underwing
carrying capacity enhancing its ground-
attack capabilities and the extra fuel it
carried allowing it to remain on station for
longer during CAS missions.

Nevertheless, only four Marine
squadrons flew the F9F-8 and F9F-8B
and none of them flew it for longer than
three years. The first was fighter unit
VMF-114, followed by VMF-311 (which
subsequently became attack squadron
VMA-311), VMA-121 and VMA-533.

The F9F-8P served with Marine
Composite Reconnaissance Squadrons
2 and 3 – VMCJ-2 and VMCJ-3 – albeit
for a relatively short time, since the
type was phased out of active service
in early 1960 as the F8U-1P Crusader
became available.

Marines training squadron VMT-1
operated the F9F-8T and the type was
later supplied to two Headquarters &
Maintenance Squadrons – H&MS-11
and H&MS-13. These would be the only
units to operate the Cougar in combat,
since each used four F9F-8Ts for fast-
FAC and airborne control duties in
Vietnam from 1966 to 1968, H&MS-11
being based at Da Nang and H&MS-
13 at Chu Lai. The back-seater would

identify enemy positions on the ground
before directing both US Marines and
their air support onto them.

Like every other naval type, under
the new tri-service naming convention
of September 1962, all surviving
Cougars received new designations.
The F9F-6 became the F-9F, F9F-6P
became RF-9F, the F9F-7 became
F-9H, the F9F-8 became F-9J, the
F9F-8B became AF-9J and the F9F-8T
became the TF-9J.

As with other early fighters, many
F-9J Cougars ended up as drones and
drone controllers, becomingQF-9Js.
The Cougar remained in service as an
advanced trainer into 1974.

DOUGLAS F3D SKYKNIGHT

It may have been slow but the Skyknight's capacious fuselage meant it could carry the electronics it needed to defeat much quicker opponents at night and ensured its longevity in the Marine Corps arsenal.

1951–1970

Experience during the Second World War had demonstrated the importance of being able to detect and destroy enemy aircraft operating after dark and the US Navy was keen to develop its own advanced night fighter. Therefore a requirement was issued in October 1945 for a radar-equipped carrier-capable jet able to reach 500mph and a ceiling of 40,000ft. Furthermore, since the pilot could not fly the aircraft and operate the radar at the same time, a second crewman was needed. The Navy stipulated that the crew should sit side by side for easy communication within a comfortable pressure cabin.

Four companies were invited to put forward proposals – Curtiss, Douglas, Fleetwings and Grumman. Douglas prepared a mock-up of its design, which was inspected in April 1946 and resulted in a contract for a trio of prototypes under the designation XF3D-1. Grumman's competing

design was chosen as a back-up with the designation XF9F-1. This would eventually lead to the highly successful F9F Panther/Cougar series.

At this time Douglas was embarking on a convention which saw many of its aircraft names begin with the word 'Sky'. There had already been the successful Skyraider and the cancelled Skypirate, which had both flown before the Second World War ended, and the experimental Skystreak had just been commissioned, so the name Skyknight was chosen for the XF3D-1 (the 'knight' presumably being a pun on 'night'). The new aircraft had a wide fuselage which provided sufficient space for a very large radome in the nose plus four cannon in the section below it. The Skyknight had straight mid-set wings which could fold upwards at their mid-way point for parking on a crowded carrier deck. Each wing had two hardpoints for drop tanks – although they could be used for bombs or rockets if necessary.

Two Westinghouse J34 turbojets were attached to the fuselage in bulky nacelles and a small second radome at the extreme rear of the aircraft housed a tail warning radar. Large air brakes were installed in the rear fuselage, similar to those of the Skyraider. The pressurised cockpit was comfortable, as specified, but it was difficult to get into and out of. The crew had to scale the right hand side of the aircraft before dropping down through an opening in the fixed upper canopy. Getting out required the same procedure to be followed in reverse.

The fixed canopy, combined with a lack of suitable ejection seats for two crew seated side by side, meant that escaping from the Skyknight in an emergency involved jumping down a tunnel which led to a hatch in the lower fuselage. Once through the hatch, the crew member would drop into empty air before manually opening their parachute.

The undercarriage was a standard tricycle arrangement but with the

▶ DOUGLAS F3D-2 SKYKNIGHT

Douglas F3D-2 Skyknight, WF-9, VMF(N)-513, Pusan West Air Base (K-1), Korea, 1953.
The first night-time radar kill of an enemy jet was achieved by a Skyknight of VMF(N)-513. On December 10, 1952, pilot Lt Joseph Corvi and radar operator Sgt Dan George locked onto a North Korean Polikarpov Po-2 biplane and shot it down without making visual contact.

▼ DOUGLAS F3D-2 SKYKNIGHT

Douglas F3D-2 Skyknight, WH-2, VMF(N)-542, Pohang Air Base (K-3), Korea, 1953.
VMF(N)-542 flew front line missions with the Skyknight in Korea but also provided training for pilots and radar intercept officers on the type.

addition of a small auxiliary tailwheel at the rear.

The first XF3D-1 took to the air with Douglas company test pilot Russell William 'Russ' Thaw at the controls on March 23, 1948. Within its nacelles were J34-WE-22 engines supplying 3000lb of thrust each. The three prototypes had to be fitted with SCR-720 radar units since the one intended for the production model aircraft, the APQ-35, was not yet available.

A period of lengthy flight testing then commenced which would, eventually, lead to an order for just 28 F3D-1 production models on June 26, 1949. By this time the 3250lb thrust J34-WE-32 was available and although this required even bigger nacelles it was worked into the design. The tailwheel was also strengthened compared to that fitted to the prototypes. Further electronic equipment was also added and the internal layout was altered.

A month earlier, on May 23, 1949, the Navy had agreed specifications for a significantly improved Skyknight with Douglas – the F3D-2. This would be fitted with the latest radar systems as well as better cockpit air conditioning, a thicker armoured windscreen, aerodynamic aids on the wings to improve rate of roll, an autopilot, and most importantly, new Westinghouse J46-WE-3 turbojets providing 4600lb of

▲ DOUGLAS F3D-2 SKYKNIGHT
Douglas F3D-2 Skyknight, LT-13, VMF(N)-531, MCAS Cherry Point, North Carolina, 1956.
VMF(N)-531 used the Skyknight until the late 1950s, flying both front line and training missions.

thrust each. These would be housed in new enlarged nacelles.

As work progressed on this variant, the first of the 28 F3D-1s flew on February 13, 1950, and was delivered to the Navy six months later. Twelve F3D-1s were modified to launch the Sparrow III missile, receiving the new designation F3D-1M. However, the missile was found to be unreliable and unable to hit manoeuvring targets. And even though the Korean War was now raging, none of these early Skyknights were sent to participate in it, being held back in the US for testing.

The first F3D-2 was ready for its first test flight in early 1951 but its engines weren't. Westinghouse had encountered serious problems with the J46 and it would eventually be cancelled. Therefore, the first F3D-2 had to be fitted with J34-WE-36s instead, providing 3400lb of thrust each, and the type would retain that engine for the remainder of its lengthy service career.

The first flight was made on February 14, 1951, and series production commenced shortly afterwards with 237 being built. The last one rolled off the production line on March 23, 1952.

DOUGLAS F3D-2Q SKYKNIGHT ▼

Douglas F3D-2Q Skyknight, CY-19, VMCJ-2, MCAS Cherry Point, North Carolina, 1958.
Several Skyknights were converted into electronic warfare aircraft; these would receive the new designation EF-10B in 1962.

The Navy never really got on with the Skyknight and although it eventually qualified for carrier operations, it would never make a full carrier deployment. The Marine Corps, on the other hand, got on famously with the aircraft.

When first sent to Korea, night fighter squadron VMF(N)-542 were equipped with F4U-5N Corsairs, F7F-3N Tigercats and a handful of Skyknights – which were then transferred to VMF(N)-513 'Flying Nightmares' in June 1952. The unit was fully operational with a dozen of them by November 1. The

following day, or rather night, the unit's Major William Stratton Jr and his radar operator Master Sergeant Hans Hoagland shot down what they claimed as a Yak-15 – though that type did not serve in Korea, and it has been speculated that what they actually destroyed was a MiG-15. Whichever type was shot down, this is believed to be the first night time jet-on-jet kill in history.

There would be another 'first' on December 10, when pilot Lt Joseph Corvi and radar operator Sgt Dan George found and destroyed a North Korean Polikarpov Po-2 biplane using a

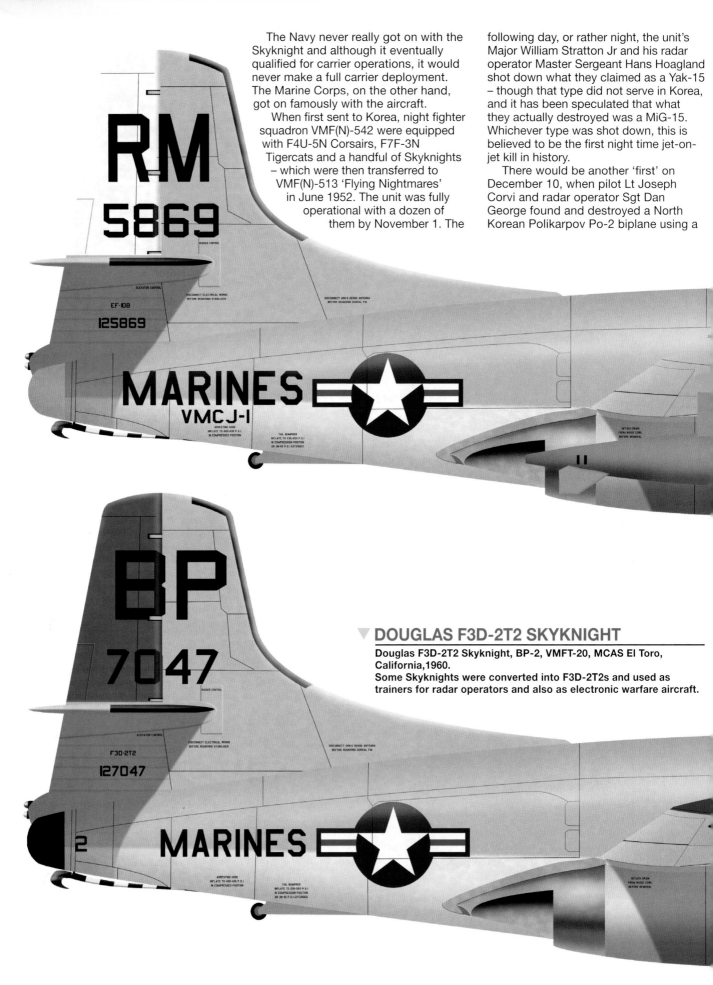

▼ DOUGLAS F3D-2T2 SKYKNIGHT

Douglas F3D-2T2 Skyknight, BP-2, VMFT-20, MCAS El Toro, California,1960.
Some Skyknights were converted into F3D-2T2s and used as trainers for radar operators and also as electronic warfare aircraft.

radar lock-on alone, no visual contact having been made.

By the end of 1952, the Flying Nightmares had 24 Skyknights and would eventually claim a total of seven further night mission jet kills for no losses to enemy action. Most of these were made while escorting Air Force B-29s, which was the unit's primary mission. Two Skyknights were lost to other causes, however.

Despite only managing a top speed of 426mph and a ceiling of 15,000ft – woefully short of the specification it was intended to meet – the Skyknight's side by side seating and spacious fuselage interior made it invaluable. Five F3D-2s were converted to become night fighter trainers under the designation F3D-2T

and another 55 became radar operator trainers, designated F3D-2T2. Another 16 had their guns removed and a longer nose fitted to house an APQ-36 radar, with the wing hardpoints being modified to carry a single Sparrow missile each. These were known as F3D-2Ms. Yet another 35 F3D-2s were converted into F3D-2Qs for electronic warfare operations. The equipment they carried enabled them to locate enemy transmitters, jam them and deploy countermeasures.

The type was redesignated F-10 in September 1962, with F3D-1s becoming F-10As, F3D-2s becoming F-10Bs, F3D-2Ms becoming MF-10Bs, the night fighter trainers becoming TF-10Bs and the F3D-2Qs becoming EF-10Bs.

VMCJ-1 flew both EF-10Bs and RF-8A Crusaders from Da Nang Air Base during the Vietnam War, starting in April 1965. These aircraft were used against enemy radar positions, with the Skyknight flying straight over a suspected radar site and then either identifying and locating it or jamming it. Attack aircraft would then be called in to knock it out. The unit flew 791 such missions over North Vietnam and Laos before being withdrawn in 1969. At least one EF-10B was shot down by a North Vietnamese SA-2 surface-to-air missile.

In addition to VMF(N)-542, VMF(N)-513 and VMCJ-1, Marine Corps units that flew the F3D-2/F-10 included VMF(N)-531, VMF(N)-46, VMC-3, VMFT(N)-20, VMCJ-2 and VMCJ-3. The last Marine Corps EF-10Bs were finally retired in May 1970.

▲ DOUGLAS EF-10B SKYKNIGHT

Douglas EF-10B Skyknight, RM-8, VMCJ-1, Da Nang Air Base, Vietnam, 1967.
VMCJ-1 Golden Hawks operated its Skyknights during the Vietnam war in the electronic warfare role. This aircraft displays several mission markings below the canopy. The Marine Corps as a whole lost five EF-10s in Vietnam during the war – one to an SA-2 surface-to-air missile and the remainder to accidents and unknown causes.

DOUGLAS F4D-1 SKYRAY

With a world-beating rate of climb and an impressive ceiling, the Skyray was probably the best interceptor in the world when it entered service in 1956. Unfortunately, it was also a dedicated day fighter with no attack capability – ensuring that its career with the Marine Corps would be brief.

EK 9068 MARINES
F4D-1 139068

AG 9196 MARINES
USS INDEPENDENCE

1957–1964

Not long after the Second World War, as previously mentioned, the advantages of a swept wing layout for improving the performance of fast jet fighters quickly became clear. Fears remained, however, that swept wings would result in unacceptably high landings speeds – making a carrier landing particularly difficult.

Having studied captured data on swept wings and tailless layouts from Germany, Douglas believed that combining these features would eliminate such difficulties. Both were therefore included in its tender when the Navy issued a requirement in 1947 for a fast-climbing high-altitude interceptor.

While Douglas engineer Edward Henry 'Ed' Heinemann and his team had initially considered a pure delta planform for their bid, they opted instead for a manta ray-like shape with thin but very deep modified delta wings, mid-mounted on the fuselage with rounded tips and with

roots extending all the way back from the cockpit to the tail. A single swept tailfin was fitted. The fuselage itself was capacious – designed to contain a single Westinghouse J40 turbojet with room to spare should a larger engine become desirable in the future. The jet was fed by intakes positioned in the wingroots on either side just aft of the cockpit.

The undercarriage was an uncomplicated tricycle arrangement – with the addition of a retractable tailwheel since the aircraft's layout meant to would take off and land at a relatively high angle of incidence. The tailhook was installed just below the tailwheel. Armament was a quartet of 20mm cannon located in the underside of the wings just inboard of the point where they folded hydraulically for carrier accommodation. There was provision for external stores too.

Having reviewed the designs tendered for its requirement, the Navy was convinced that Douglas's was the best and awarded the company a contract

for two prototypes, with the designation XF4D-1, on December 16, 1948. Given its shape and the company's ongoing 'Sky' naming convention, Douglas had little difficulty in coming up with the name 'Skyray' for the type.

A mock-up was built and inspected in March 1949 and work on the prototypes progressed quickly. Unfortunately, the same could not be said of the J40-WE-8, which Westinghouse was struggling to complete. Therefore, the first Skyrays were fitted with Allison's J35-A-17. This produced a meagre 4900lb of thrust compared to the 11,600lb projected for the J40-WE-8.

Testing commenced with the first XF4D-1 being flown for the first time by Douglas test pilot Larry Peyton on January 23, 1951. Early on it was evident that the Skyray suffered from control problems and tail buffeting. The former was resolved by redesigning the elevons and the latter was addressed by reshaping the tail cone.

▼ DOUGLAS F4D-1 SKYRAY
Douglas F4D-1 Skyray, EK-3, VMF(AW)-114, MCAS Cherry Point, North Carolina, 1958.
The F4D-1 was the first Marine aircraft capable of reaching supersonic speed in level flight.

▼ DOUGLAS F4D-1 SKYRAY
Douglas F4D-1 Skyray, AG-105, VMF(AW)-115, USS *Independence* (CVA-62), 1962.
VMF(AW)-115 was the first USMC squadron to operate the F4D, receiving its first example of the type in 1957. Although usually based at MCAS Cherry Point, VMF(AW)-115 was deployed aboard USS *Independence* in 1962 from April 19 to August 27.

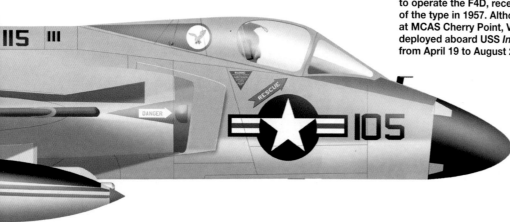

Two working J40-WE-6 units – a development version of the J40-WE-8 – were received by Douglas in mid-1952 and installed in the two XF4D-1s, but reliability issues were immediately encountered and their power output was still only 7500lb. It would be another year before the long-awaiting J40-WE-8s were finally delivered, by which time a year had been wasted.

Even the J40-WE-8 fell short of Westinghouse's original promises, providing 10,900lb of thrust with afterburner, but this was deemed sufficient. With one of these installed and piloted by Lieutenant Commander James B Verdin, the second XF4D-1 set a new air speed record of 752.9mph on October 3, 1953 – which made it the first US Navy aircraft ever to go supersonic.

Interviewed about this feat later, Verdin said: "Douglas had its high priced help

DOUGLAS F4D-1 SKYRAY ▼

Douglas F4D-1 Skyray, WH-8, VMF(AW)-542, MCAS El Toro, California, 1959.
The Skyrays of VMF(AW)-542 Tigers made two extended deployments to Atsugi, Japan, between August 1959 and November 1963 but their home base was MCAS El Toro.

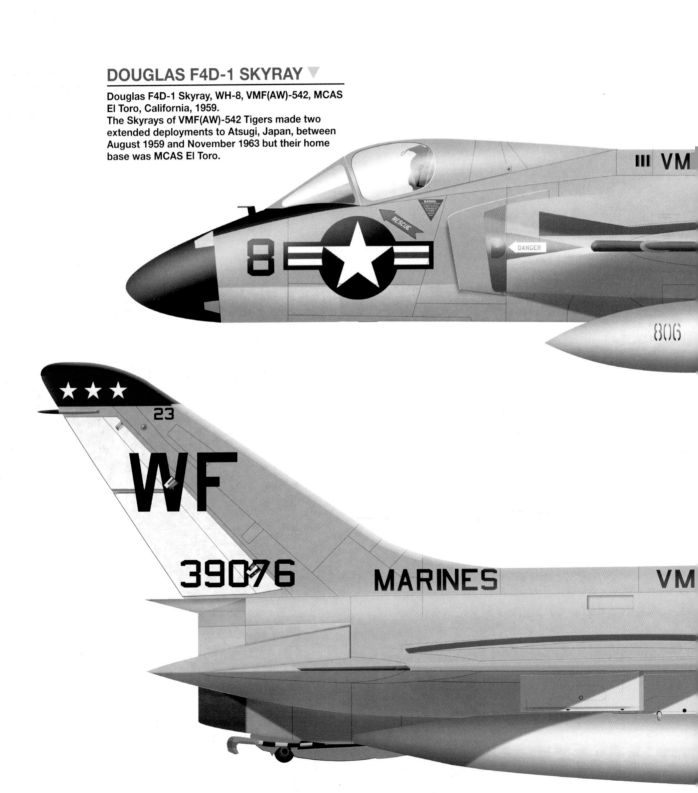

there at the course, and they iced my fuel for the Skyray while I took a look at the course from a Grumman Cougar. They ice the fuel because that shrinks it and you can pack more in. We towed her out to the starting line to save the stuff. Didn't even use blocks on the wheels after the engine was started. Just started rolling. I was in the air a little over a minute after the engine started, and headed for the measured course, 40 miles away.

"It was marked for me by smudge pots and burning tyres, and orange-red markers to tell me when to turn off my afterburner, which eats fuel like crazy. About five miles short of the line I was doing 620 and turned on the afterburner. It gave me another hundred miles an hour right away, and I held her steady and low over the course. It doesn't take long, about nine seconds for the just under two miles."

▼ DOUGLAS F4D-1 SKYRAY

Douglas F4D-1 Skyray, WF-23, VMF(AW)-513, NAS Atsugi, Japan, 1962.
VMF(AW)-513 operated F4Ds while deployed to Japan. After heading back to the US it would be re-equipped with F-4 Phantoms.

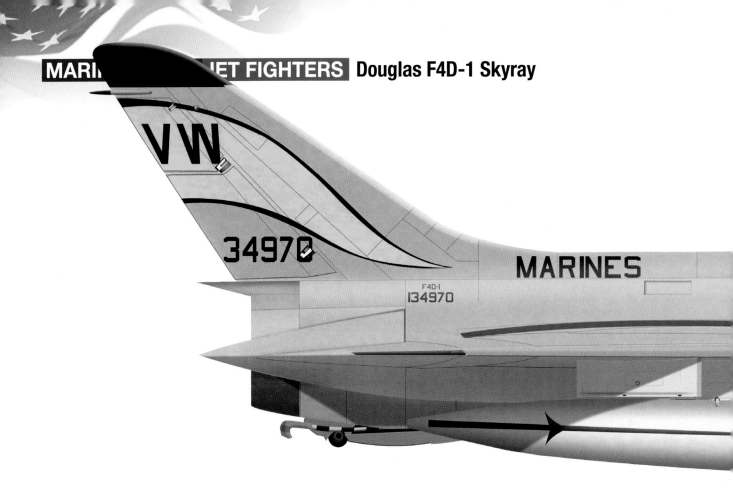

DOUGLAS F4D-1 SKYRAY ▼

Douglas F4D-1 Skyray, 7K-101, Naval Air Reserve Training Unit (NARTU) Olathe, Kansas, 1964. Reserve units used former USMC and US Navy front line aircraft to train personnel of both services. They were the final destination for several Marines Skyrays which were then flown well into the 1960s.

Having taken the record from British test pilot Mike Lithgow, who'd hit 735.7mph in a Supermarine Swift F.4 only a week earlier on September 26, Verdin's own record fell in less than a month when USAF chief test pilot Frank K Everest reached 755.1mph in an F-100. Verdin died on January 13, 1955, when his parachute failed to open after he'd ejected from a YA4D-1 Skyhawk.

Despite this record-breaking success, it was clear that the J40 had major problems which would prevent it from reaching series production, so Pratt & Whitney's J57-P-2 was specified for the production Skyray instead. This could produce 10,200lb of thrust or 14,500lb with afterburner. And this was then changed to the J57-P-8 which, while it only gave 8700lb dry, provided 16,000lb with afterburner.

Fitted with enlarged intakes but otherwise looking very similar to the prototypes, the first production F4D-1 flew on June 5, 1954. The series variant had an AN/APQ-50 radar in its nose and could carry rocket pods, drop tanks or Sidewinders on six underwing hard points and one centreline fuselage position. Despite this early start, Skyray deliveries to the Navy did not begin until April 16,

▼ DOUGLAS F4D-1 SKYRAY

Douglas F4D-1 Skyray, VW-15, VMF(AW)-314, MCAS El Toro, California,1960.
While flying the Skyray, VMF(AW)-314 Black Knights made numerous deployments across the Far East as well as aboard the fast attack carriers USS *Hancock* and USS *Ticonderoga*.

1956, and the Marine Corps did not receive any until 1957. During its relatively brief period in service with the USMC it would equip VMF-113, VMF-114, VMF-115, VMF-215, VMF-314, VMF-513, VMFA-531, VMF(AW)-542 and evaluation unit VX-3.

A total of 419 F4D-1 Skyrays were built and there were no variants, although an F4D-2 was planned and would eventually

appear as the F5D-1 Skylancer, of which only prototypes were built.

In 1962, surviving F4D-1s received the designation F-6A. Under this number it continued to fly with Reserve units into 1964 before it was finally phased out. The last unit to operate Skyrays on active duty was VMF(AW)-542 'Tigers' from Atsugi in Japan. They were rotated back to the US in November 1963.

Despite having an incredible ability to climb at high-speed, setting new time-to-climb records in 1958, the Skyray simply did not possess the multirole capability demanded by the Marine Corps. It was only marginally effective in bad weather, its straight line speed was quickly topped by newer fighters and it was evidently difficult to fly too. Indeed, much better aircraft were just around the corner for the USMC.

VOUGHT F-8 CRUSADER

Starting out as a dedicated day fighter, the F-8 matured into the Marines' first true multirole combat aircraft – just as capable of fighting off enemy planes as it was of supporting Marines on the ground.

DC

3812

MARINES
VMF-122

F8U-1
143812

AK

5454

MARINES
VMF-251

F8U-1E
145454

1957–1976

The high turnover of aircraft types seen during the Second World War had continued into the 1950s, with the Korean War effectively igniting a new arms race between east and west. It was business as usual for the US Navy to keep commissioning new aircraft in the full knowledge that these would last only a few years before replacements were needed to retain a performance edge.

The F-8 Crusader was the first postwar fighter to break this cycle – with supersonic performance right out of the box and an airframe that could be incrementally upgraded and improved to keep pace with technological advancements.

Its story begins with a September 1952 US Navy requirement for a carrier fighter capable of Mach 1.2 that would also be manoeuvrable in combat and reliable during extended operations at sea. At the time, McDonnell was struggling with its F3H-1 Demon and Douglas with the F4D-1 Skyray. Both types had been specified with Westinghouse's J40 engine, which was suffering from what would turn out to be insurmountable technical problems.

Vought too had been working through issues with an advanced swept-wing type – the F7U-1 Cutlass. And like the other companies it had learned valuable lessons while doing so. Unlike those other companies and their designs, Vought realised that the Cutlass layout

had had little potential for development. So when the Navy called for its next-generation air superiority fighter, the company put everything it had learned into a completely new layout where most of its competitors offered upgraded versions of their existing designs.

McDonnell offered an upgraded F3H Demon and North American came up with an upgraded F-100 Super Sabre, which it called the 'Super Fury'. Grumman chose the same path as Vought with its F11F Tiger, which, though it was very distantly related to the F9F Cougar (with prototypes initially being designated XF9F-9), was actually a completely new aircraft.

Vought's design, designated V-383, made use of lightweight magnesium

▼ VOUGHT F8U-1 (F-8A) CRUSADER

Vought F8U-1 (F-8A) Crusader, DC-16, VMF-122, MCAS Beaufort, South Carolina, 1958.
VMF-122 was the first USMC squadron to operate the Vought Crusader. Early variants featured a retractable rocket pack but this was deleted from later F-8s.

▼ VOUGHT F8U-1E (F-8B) CRUSADER

Vought F8U-1E (F-8B) Crusader, AK-213, VMF-251, USS *Shangri-la* (CVA-38), 1962.
The F8U-1E (later redesignated F-8B) had limited all-weather capability thanks to the new AN/APS-67 radar.

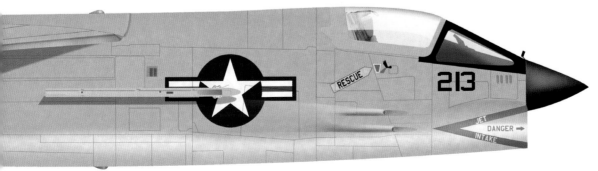

▼ VOUGHT F-8C CRUSADER

Vought F-8C Crusader, WU-15, VMF-334, MCAS El Toro, California, 1966.
This F-8C displays a striking colour scheme, something commonly seen on Marine aircraft until the late 1970s. The F-8C featured several engine and equipment improvements and had ventral fins installed to improved flight characteristics.

▼ VOUGHT F8U-2 (F-8C) CRUSADER

Vought F8U-2 (F-8C) Crusader, WS-202, VMF-323, USS *Lexington* (CVA-16), 1962.
Land-based in California, VMF-323 made several aircraft carrier deployments with the F-8, including aboard the USS *Lexington.*

alloy and titanium in limited quantities to provide extra structural strength and its fuselage was 'area ruled' for supersonic flight.

Within the long fuselage was a single Pratt & Whitney J57-P-11 turbojet, fed by a substantial chin intake beneath the aircraft's radome nose. This would provide 9700lb of dry thrust or 14,800lb with afterburner. The radome would house an AN/APG-30 radar gunsight, rather than a full radar system, for three 'T-160' 20mm cannon in the lower lip of the intake. Alternatively, or additionally, the aircraft could be armed with 60 FFAR 2in rockets.

The low nosewheel and mainwheels of the tricycle undercarriage folded into the fuselage – so low in fact that later, in service, the Crusader earned the nickname 'Gator' since its belly was so close to the ground.

Within the cockpit, the pilot had good visibility upwards, to the sides, and down while seated on an ejection seat that would be designed and built by Vought itself.

The V-383's party piece, however, was its wings. These sat on top of the fuselage as a single structural piece which hinged at the rear and could be jacked up seven degrees at the front by hydraulics (there was

also a pneumatic backup in case the hydraulics failed to operate). Raising the wings this way for both takeoff and landing meant the pilot did not have to suffer the reduced visibility which came with pitching the aircraft's nose up for either manoeuvre.

The wings assumed a high angle of attack, while the remainder of the aircraft stayed level. The linkage also lowered the ailerons and leading edge flaps by 25 degrees – which automatically decreased take-off and approach speed by providing additional lift. The wingtips could be folded vertically for carrier storage and the wings themselves had a 5% anhedral.

In addition to the V-383, Vought also tendered the V-384. This was a very similar design but powered by a Wright J65 variant with a projected maximum thrust of 11,000lb. The lower thrust meant that the V-384 had to be smaller overall. Its fuselage was 48ft 3in long, compared to 54ft 5.5in for the V-383, and wingspan was 34ft 3in compared to the V-383's 35ft 8in. The variable wing mechanism remained the same however.

Vought received a contract to develop the V-383 in May 1953 and two prototypes were ordered on June 29 under the designation XF8U-1. As work progressed, the design was altered somewhat and details previously left vague were fleshed out. The three 20mm cannon became four and they were repositioned so that two were installed on either side of the fuselage below the cockpit, well back from the intake.

The underside of the aircraft housed a retractable rocket pack which could accommodate thirty-two 2.75in 'Mighty Mouse' FFARs plus a large hydraulic air

▼ VOUGHT F-8K CRUSADER

Vought F-8K Crusader, MC-5, VMF-351, NAS Atlanta, Georgia, 1974. VMF-351 was a reserve unit. Several variants of the Crusader were re-manufactured resulting in new designations; F-8Ks were F-8Cs upgraded with new radars, engines and new weapons capabilities.

brake and an arrestor hook to the rear which could be retracted into the fuselage.

The whole rear of the aircraft could be detached and slid away to provide full access to the engine for maintenance or replacement. On the right side of the fuselage, Vought added a pop-out intake for a Ram Air Turbine or 'RAT'. When this was activated, slipstream air entered and span a small turbine to generate emergency backup power for the aircraft's systems.

The first prototype XF8U-1 was rolled out in February 1955 and its first flight was made on March 25 with Vought chief experimental test pilot John W Konrad at the controls. Konrad found

the aircraft responsive and took it above Mach 1 during that initial test flight. The second prototype joined the first on June 12 and the company named the aircraft 'Crusader'.

Further testing revealed no serious problems and manufacture of the F8U-1 therefore commenced quickly. The first production example was rolled out on September 20, 1955, fitted with the somewhat improved J57-P-12. From the 31st aircraft onwards, this was changed to the significantly more powerful J57-P-4A, which offered 10,900lb of dry thrust or 16,000lb with afterburner – an increase of 1200lb on the -11 and -12 models. The production F8U-1 was

also able to carry a pair of Sidewinder missiles on rails located on the fuselage sides just forward of the wing roots.

Carrier qualification trials began on USS *Forrestal* in January 1955 and US Navy front line units began to receive Crusaders on December 28, 1956. The first Marine Corps squadron to receive them was VMF-122 in December 1957.

A total of 318 of these early F8U-1s were constructed from an order of 448 (see below for what became of the other 130) and the 32nd example would be modified to create a reconnaissance version – the F8U-1P. The four cannon were removed and five camera stations were added to the underside of the

▲ VOUGHT F-8E CRUSADER

Vought F-8E Crusader, WT-4, VMF(AW)-232, Da Nang air base, Vietnam, 1967.
VMF-232 flew combat missions in Vietnam from late 1966 until late 1967, when it returned to the USA to be equipped with the F-4 Phantom II. F-8Es could carry a variety of weapons, both on the fuselage and wing pylons. A total of 21 USMC F-8s were lost during the war, plus one RF-8.

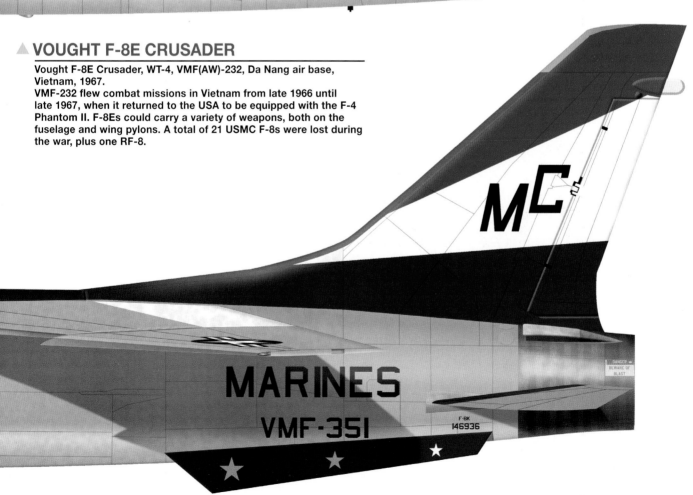

VOUGHT F-8D CRUSADER ▽

Vought F-8D Crusader, VM-9, VMF(AW)-451, MCAS Beaufort, South Carolina, 1964.
Aircraft from VMF(AW)-451 participated in Operation Highboy V in May 1964. This was a transatlantic crossing from the USA to Spain which made use of in-flight refuelling. F-8s were equipped with one retractable probe located on the left-side fuselage.

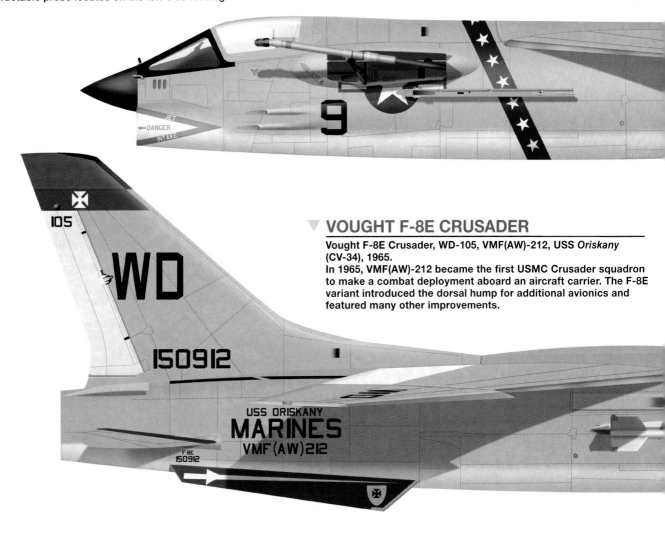

▽ VOUGHT F-8E CRUSADER

Vought F-8E Crusader, WD-105, VMF(AW)-212, USS *Oriskany* (CV-34), 1965.
In 1965, VMF(AW)-212 became the first USMC Crusader squadron to make a combat deployment aboard an aircraft carrier. The F-8E variant introduced the dorsal hump for additional avionics and featured many other improvements.

VOUGHT F-8K CRUSADER ▽

Vought F-8K Crusader, 5A-11, VMF-321, NAS Anacostia, Washington DC, 1973.
VMF-321, a Marine Air Reserve squadron, operated the Crusader from 1965 until 1973.

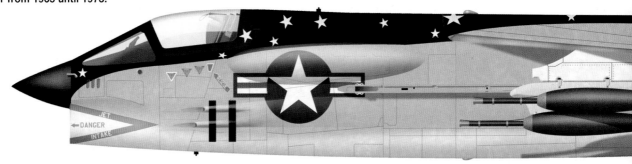

forward fuselage. Two square windows were fitted on each side of the aircraft, three on the underside and one more, facing forward, was part of a pod installed directly below the cockpit. Another change was a shortened tailfin for better aerodynamic performance. The first F8U-1P prototype flew on December 17, 1957, and 144 were built overall.

Unusually, the Crusader could be flown faster than the manufacturer had specified. Pilots could achieve Mach 1.7, where Vought had only claimed a top speed of Mach 1.4. On the downside, the F8U-1 could be hard to recover if it entered a spin – and in spite of the clever wing mechanic it was still a difficult aircraft to land safely due to a high approach speed.

Pilots had to remember to retract the under-fuselage air brake before touchdown – and the hydraulics for it had a habit of leaking, which meant that it sometimes hung down anyway. These issues combined resulted in a high accident rate – an incredible 87% of F8U-1s suffering a mishap at some point.

The next major variant was the F8U-1E, in which the AN/APG-30 radar gunsight was swapped for a more useful AN/APS-67 radar system (the 'E' in the aircraft's designation stood for 'Electronics'). This meant a more capacious nosecone was necessary but apart from that the F8U-1E was similar to the original F8U-1. The last 130 Crusaders from the original order of 448 were built to F8U-1E standard, with the first one flying on September 3, 1958.

THE LAST CRUSADER

Even as the F8U-1E project was getting under way, Vought was already hard at work on what it called 'Crusader II'. This version of the aircraft, which would receive the less grandiose-sounding F8U-2 official designation, had the new J57-P-16 from Pratt & Whitney. This was slightly down on power without afterburner at 10,700lb of thrust, but once the afterburner was fired up it provided 16,900lb and speeds not too far away from Mach 2.

Vought's own ejection seat was deleted from the design and replaced with the new Martin-Baker Mark 5 model, two new intakes were added on top of the tailcone to provide afterburner cooling and a pair of ventral strakes were installed below the tail for extra stability.

Wingspan was reduced by 6in and the fuselage single-missile rails were replaced by new Y-shaped rails which could carry two missiles each. In service, however, F8U-2s still only tended to carry one missile per side.

The first F8U-2 prototype, effectively just a standard F8U-1 with the new engine fitted, flew for the first time in December 1957 – nine months before the first F8U-1E. A more heavily modified F8U-1 followed a month later to allow testing of other F8U-2 features.

▼ VOUGHT F-8E CRUSADER

Vought F-8E Crusader, DB-3, VMF(AW)-235, Da Nang air base, Vietnam, 1965.
VMF(AW)-235's Crusaders operated in Vietnam over the course of several deployments from 1965 to 1968. This aircraft carries Zuni rockets and bombs.

▼ VOUGHT F-8K CRUSADER

Vought F-8K Crusader, 5W-21, VMF-511 NAS Willow Grove, Pennsylvania, 1971.
VMF-511 was a reserve squadron. All Crusaders feature a variable incidence wing for improved take-off and landing performance.

▼ VOUGHT F-8E CRUSADER

Vought F-8E Crusader, DR-1, VMF-312, NAS Miami, Florida, 1964.
VMF-312 operated Crusaders from 1959 until 1966; its next aircraft was the F-4 Phantom II.

Nevertheless, the first F8U-2 still rolled off the production line ahead of the first production F8U-1E in August 1958. A total of 187 had been built by September 1960. It was next decided that a dedicated night fighter Crusader was needed and by now an even better J57 was available – the J57-P-20, offering 18,000lb of thrust with afterburner.

The F8U-2N had this new -20 engine and the belly rocket pack, which had long been sealed up on previous Crusader variants, was finally deleted. This freed up space for extra internal fuel capacity, better radar and fire control systems, and the addition of an autopilot. Just above the nosecone, a nodule was fitted housing an infrared search and track sensor.

The F8U-2N first flew on February 16, 1960, and a total of 152 were built, with production ending in early 1962.

There followed one final new-build version of the Crusader – the F8U-2NE. Even greater night and all-weather capability was provided with the installation of the new AN/APQ-94 search and fire control radar and underwing pylons were added, enabling carriage of up to 5000lb in external stores. Typical loads included bombs, rockets or air-to-surface missiles such as the AGM-12 Bullpup. The guidance systems for the latter were crammed into a new centre-wing hump.

Offering a significant leap forward in capability, the F8U-2NE had the second largest production run of all Crusader variants with 286 made.

Plans were laid for a two-seat Crusader trainer – the F8U-1T 'Twosader' – and the 77th F8U-1 was modified to create a prototype with its fuselage stretched 2ft to create the extra cockpit. But despite this taking to the air in 1962 and undergoing tests, the Navy declined to make the purchase.

When the tri-service designation system was introduced in September 1962, with many Crusaders of all variants still in service, the F8U-1 became the F-8A, the F8U-1P became the RF-8A, the F8U-1E was the F-8B, the F8U-2 became the F-8C, the F8U-2N became the F-8D and the F8U-2NE became the F-8E.

By 1963, Chance Vought was the 8th largest defence contractor in the United States but its success had attracted unwanted attention. Ling-Temco, a conglomerate led by the incredibly aggressive and acquisitive Jim Ling, with sales that were only half those of Vought, started buying up its stock in 1960 – borrowing money and going deep into debt to do so.

By early 1961, Ling had more than 10% of Vought stock and continued to offer large sums for every share he could get his hands on. Within two months, Ling held nearly 40% of Vought's stock and was able to force a hostile takeover.

The Change Vought F8U Crusader now became the Ling-Temco-Vought (LTV) F8U Crusader.

VOUGHT F-8D CRUSADER ▼

Vought F-8D Crusader, DN-16, VMF(AW)-333, MCAS Beaufort, South Carolina, 1966.
VMF-333 added All Weather (AW) to its designation when operating the F-8D variant of the Crusader. F-8Ds had all weather capability thanks to improved avionics. The squadron saw action during the Cuban Missile Crisis using earlier model Crusaders.

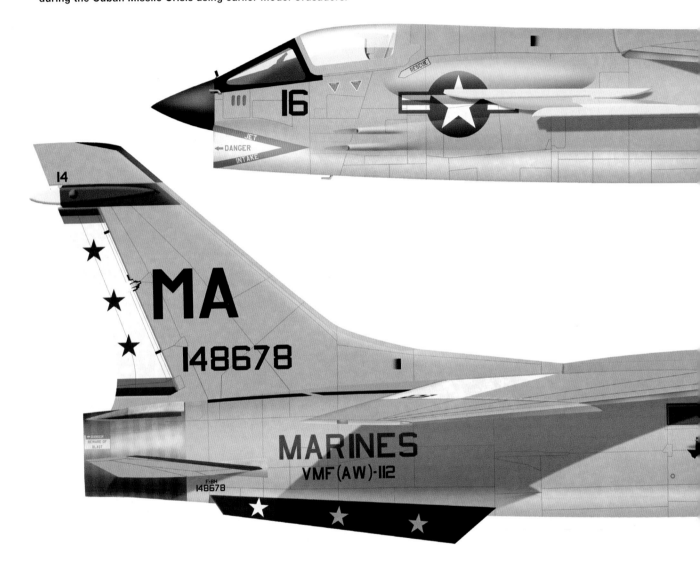

VOUGHT F-8U-1P (RF-8A) CRUSADER ▼

Vought F-8U-1P (RF-8A) Crusader, CY-33, VMCJ-2, MCAS Cherry Point, North Carolina, 1962.
The RF-8A was the initial Crusader photographic reconnaissance variant. VMCJ-2 resulted from the merger of VMJ-2 and VMC-2.

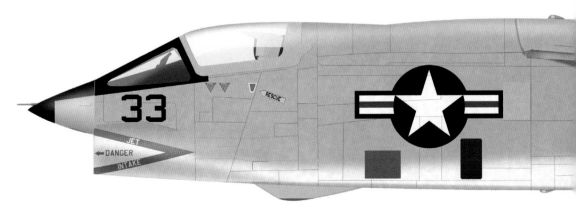

▼ VOUGHT F-8H CRUSADER

Vought F-8H Crusader, MA-14, VMF(AW)-112, NAS Dallas, Texas, 1975. VMF-112 was a reserve unit operating several different F-8 variants up to 1975. F-8Hs were upgraded F-8Ds.

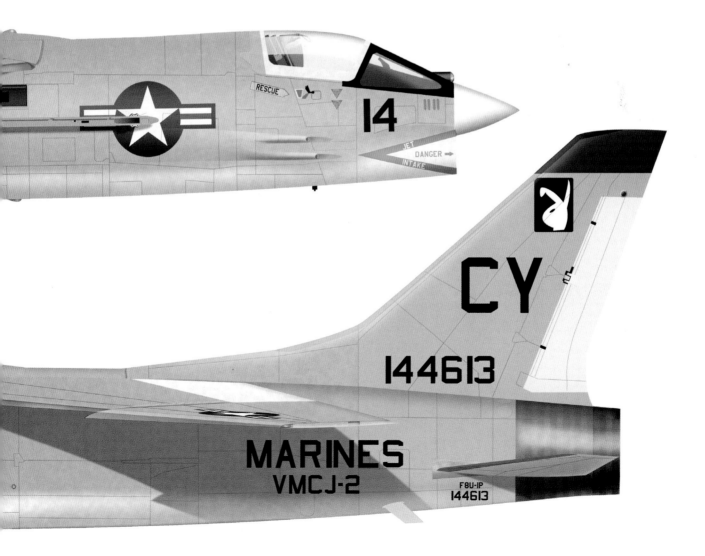

VOUGHT RF-8A CRUSADER ▼

Vought RF-8A Crusader, RM-16, VMCJ-1, MCAS El Toro, California, 1960.
RF-8As of VMCJ-1 operated during the Tonkin Gulf Incident, continuing to fly combat missions over south-east Asia for several more years thereafter.

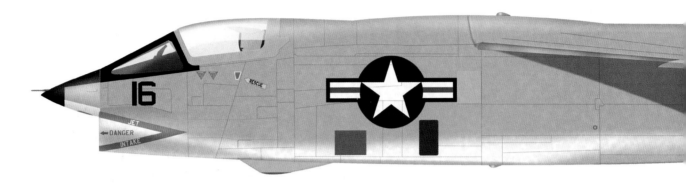

VOUGHT RF-8A CRUSADER ▼

Vought RF-8A Crusader, 7K-121, VMJ-4, NAS Olathe, Kansas, 1968.
VMJ-4 was the only Marines reserve photographic reconnaissance squadron.

VOUGHT RF-8G CRUSADER ▼

Vought RF-8G Crusader, TN-21, VMCJ-3, MCAS El Toro, California, 1961.
RF-8Gs were upgraded RF-8As featuring new electronic equipment and ventral fins.

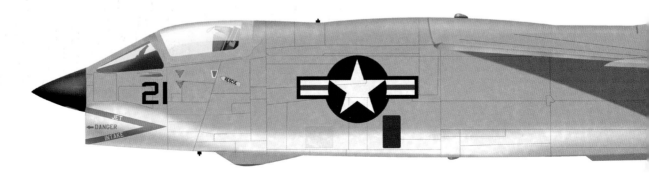

VIETNAM

An auto-throttle system was retrofitted to all remaining Crusaders from 1964, making the aircraft easier to land by smoothing out the throttle response. This would be the beginning of an extensive refurbishment programme for all F-8s, except for the F-8As. Beginning in 1965, the newer variants received stronger wings with hardpoints as standard plus new landing gear derived from that of Vought's own A-7A Corsair II – including a longer nosewheel leg.

As the Crusaders were upgraded, they received new designations. The RF-8A became the RF-8G (73 aircraft), the F-8D became the F-8H (89 aircraft), the F-8E became the F-8J (136 aircraft), the F-8C became the F-8K (87 aircraft) and the F-8B became the F-8L (61 aircraft).

The Crusader had matured just in time for the Vietnam War. Marine fighter squadron VMF(AW)-212 Lancers, flying F-8Es, were assigned to Attack Carrier Air Wing Sixteen (CVW-16) aboard the carrier USS *Oriskany* for deployment to Vietnam from April 5 to December 16, 1965. And from that month on, VMF(AW)-312 was stationed at Da Nang flying close air support and interdiction missions against ground targets. They would soon be joined by VMF(AW)-232 and VMF(AW)-235 – all flying F-8s.

A wide range of missions ensued, from dropping bombs on enemy forces using the Ho Chi Minh Trail to helicopter escort, attacking SAM sites, close air support and suppression of enemy fire during extraction missions for downed US aircrew.

At any given time, a number of F-8s from each unit would 'sit alert' – waiting by the runway fully armed and with full fuel tanks so they could take off at a moment's notice to provide air strikes in support of ground forces.

During the Tet Offensive in January 1968, VMF(AW)-235 flew 681 sorties during which it delivered 1000 tons of napalm, bombs, rockets and cannon shells. Marines on the ground valued the F-8s above attack helicopters because they could bring a heavier weight of firepower to the fight.

After three years of heavy combat, and having flown 20,955 sorties, the Marine F-8s finally left South Vietnam in May 1968. Twenty-two had been lost during their time in-theatre.

That year, newer Crusaders were fitted with Martin-Baker Mark 7 ejection seats which finally gave the aircraft's pilots zero-zero ejection as an emergency option. A number of the older F-8s were converted into drone controllers as DF-8As and drones as QF-8As and DQF-8As in the late 1960s.

During its front line career, 17 different Marine squadrons flew the type and VMF(AW)-235 was the last to transition to the F-4 Phantom II in September 1968. Marine Corps Reserve units would continue to fly it until 1976.

MCDONNELL DOUGLAS F-4 PHANTOM II

The excellent F-4 Phantom II picked up where the Crusader left off as the mainstay Marine Corps multirole fighter. Adaptable and highly capable, it would remain in service throughout the 1960s, 1970s, 1980s and into the 1990s.

The twin-engine McDonnell Douglas F-4 Phantom II was a descendant of the single-engine F3H Demon. As the Demon prototypes were undergoing carrier trials in August 1953, McDonnell embarked on a new project to further develop the aircraft using the latest technology.

The project was designated Model 98 and this encompassed five different approaches. Model 98A would be essentially a Demon fitted with a Wright J67 instead of the Westinghouse J40 it had originally been designed for. 98B was a reimagining of the Demon that could

be either a fighter or reconnaissance platform, powered by either two Wright J65s or two General Electric J79s and with enlarged wings.

The twin-engine Models 98C and 98D both had the same engine options but the 98C had an entirely new delta wing while the 98D had new straight wings. Model 98E had a delta wing like Model 98C but larger and thinner.

Any of the five designs could be a single or two-seater, and any could be fitted with up to nine external stores stations. Confident that these concepts had outstanding potential for development, McDonnell submitted them

to the Navy as an unsolicited proposal for a 'Super Demon' on September 19, 1953, and found the service receptive.

Model 98B was selected as the most promising layout, in single-seater form and with near-delta swept wings, and the company received a contract for a full-scale mock-up during early 1954. It was initially decided that the new aircraft should be an attacker and the design was changed to allow for up to 11 external stations, supplementing four 20mm cannon in the nose.

An inspection of the mock-up on October 18, 1954, resulted in an order for two prototypes under the designation

1960-1992

▼ MCDONNELL DOUGLAS F-4B PHANTOM II

McDonnell Douglas F-4B Phantom II, EC-7, VMFA-531, Da Nang air base, Vietnam, 1965.
VMFA-531's Phantoms arrived in Vietnam in April of 1965, thus becoming the first land-based USMC jet squadron to operate there.

▼ MCDONNELL DOUGLAS F-4J PHANTOM II

McDonnell Douglas F-4J Phantom II, AJ-201, VMFA-333, USS America (CV-66), 1972.
Major Lee T 'Bear' Lasseter and his RIO Captain John D Cummings of VMFA-333 Fighting Shamrocks made one of only three USMC Vietnam war MiG kills on September 11, 1972, when they shot down a black MiG-21 over North Vietnam, near Hanoi. Their F-4J was hit by an SA-2 SAM moments later and they were eventually forced to eject over the ocean.

▼ MCDONNELL DOUGLAS F-4B PHANTOM II

McDonnell Douglas F-4B Phantom II, VW-13, VMFA-314, Chu Lai air base, Vietnam, 1968.
VMFA-314 was the first USMC squadron to be equipped with the F-4 Phantom II and would fly them in combat over Vietnam.

MCDONNELL DOUGLAS F-4B PHANTOM II ▽

McDonnell Douglas F-4B Phantom II, VE-3, VMFA-115, Da Nang air base, Vietnam, 1969.
VMFA-115 saw extensive combat over Vietnam, participating in Linebacker missions, among others, over North Vietnam.

MCDONNELL DOUGLAS F-4B PHANTOM II ▽

McDonnell Douglas F-4B Phantom II, WH-9, VMFA-542, Da Nang air base, Vietnam, 1966.
Phantoms could rely on external fuel tanks and their retractable in-flight refuelling probe to extend range. VMFA-542 was engaged in combat in the Vietnam theatre from 1965 to 1970.

YAH-1. However, Douglas's A-4 Skyhawk was already proving to be more than capable of fulfilling the Navy's ground-attack needs. The F3H-2N Demon, on the other hand, was starting to enter service as an all-weather fleet defence fighter equipped with the latest missile technology. The 'Super Demon' would therefore be its replacement.

The Navy specified that the new aircraft should now be a two-seater and a pure missile platform from the outset. Two General Electric J79-GE-3As would power it and it was redesignated YF4H-1. McDonnell gave it the name 'Phantom II', harking back to the 'Phantom' name previously used for the company's FH-1.

The engine's intakes were on either side of the fuselage next to the back-seater's position and the engines themselves were set low down in the rear fuselage. The thin-section delta wing would have 45° leading edge sweepback and the outer wings were angled up by 12° to cure a lateral instability problem revealed by wind tunnel testing. A 'dogtooth' was also given to the leading edge for better control at high angles of attack and for that same reason the tailplanes were given an unusual 23.25° anhedral.

Given the Navy's demand for a fighter armed only with missiles, the four cannon originally planned were deleted and instead there would be four AIM-7 Sparrows in semi-recessed bays under the fuselage plus Sidewinders on the underwing pylons if required. The nose would house an AN/APG-50 radar unit for guiding the Sparrows. It would be the first US fighter to be armed only with missiles.

The first YF4H-1 Phantom was taken up for its flight debut by McDonnell test pilot Robert C Little on May 27, 1958, and testing soon identified a boundary layer issue with the intakes. As a result, 12,500 small holes were added to the inner intake doors to allow boundary layer air extraction. In addition, a new system was installed where air from the compressors could be blown across the leading edge slats and trailing edge flaps to improve their performance.

The F4H-1 defeated Vought's rival XF8U-3 Crusader III in fly-offs during December 1958 and the Navy's initial order for 20 pre-production models

MCDONNELL DOUGLAS F-4J PHANTOM II ▽

McDonnell Douglas F-4J Phantom II, VM-14, VMFA-451, MCAS Beaufort,
South Carolina, 1974.
The F-4J was an upgraded variant of the F-4B, featuring an improved
engine, avionics, aerodynamics and other updates. VMFA-451 Warlords
flew Phantoms for 20 years – from 1968 to 1987.

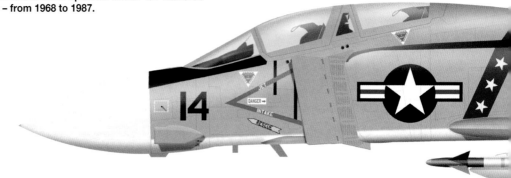

MCDONNELL DOUGLAS F-4J PHANTOM II ▽

McDonnell Douglas F-4J Phantom II, VMFA-232, MCAS Iwakuni, Japan, 1976.
For the 200th anniversary of the American Revolution, in 1976, several
military aircraft were given commemorative colour schemes – among them
was this Phantom from VMFA-232.

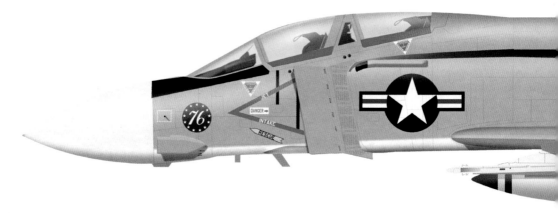

▼ MCDONNELL DOUGLAS F-4J PHANTOM II

McDonnell Douglas F-4J Phantom II, DB-4, VMFA-235, MCAS Kaneohe Bay, Hawaii, 1973.
VMF-235 Death Angels flew more than 6000 combat sorties in F-8s supporting 22 major operations in Vietnam. They were the last active duty F-8 squadron by May 1968 and left the theatre shortly thereafter, relocating to Hawaii. Here they were redesignated VMFA-235 and re-equipped with the F-4.

was increased to 45. These aircraft, designated F4H-1F, would be powered by the J79-GE-2 or J79-GE-2A, an interim engine supplied by General Electric while the J79-GE-8 was prepared for full scale production. At the same time, the F4H-1 design underwent more revisions. These included a raised cockpit canopy for better visibility, new fixed and variable ramps for the intake ducts, and an increased diameter nose to house the larger AN/APQ-72 radar.

By the end of 1959 it was becoming clear what a hot-rod the new Phantom was. The second YF4H-1 prototype took part in Project Top Flight on December 6, 1959, to set a world record altitude of 98,557ft and on February 15, 1960, the fourth F4H-1F pre-production model was used to make the Phantom's first aircraft carrier launch and recovery on USS *Independence*.

The full production model F4H-1's J79-GE-8 engines provided an eye-watering 17,000lb of thrust each with afterburner and the aircraft's intake ramps needed modification to suit them. In addition, space-saving refinements within the fuselage, compared to the F4H-1Fs, allowed an internal fuel capacity increase.

As well as the four Sparrows positioned under the fuselage, the F4H-1 was the first Phantom able to carry four rail-mounted AIM-9 Sidewinders on the inner wing pylons. US Navy squadrons received the Phantom first, with VF-74 getting its first F4H-1 on July 8, 1961. Early aircraft would be used to set further records – with Lt H Hardisty and Lt E H DeEsch using an F4H-1F to set a low altitude record of 902.769mph during Operation Sageburner on August 28, 1961.

The USAF was loaned 29 F4H-1s for trials in October that year, with the first two receiving 'F-110A' markings. Navy pilot Lt Col Robert B Robinson set a new world air speed record of 1606.3mph in the second YF4H-1 during Operation Skyburner at Edwards AFB on November 22. Between February and April 1962, eight time-to-climb records were set by various pilots during Operation High Jump using various F4H-1s.

The Marine Corps would finally receive its first F4H-1s in June 1962, with VMFA-314 Black Knights becoming the first operational Phantom squadron at Marine Corps Air Station El Toro, California. Just three months later, the new tri-service designation system would see the pre-production F4H-1F type becoming the F-4A and the production F4H-1 becoming the F-4B.

US Navy squadrons were by now making carrier deployments with the Phantom. Notably, VF-142 and VF-143 aboard USS *Constellation* escorted A-4 Skyhawks during Operation Pierce Arrow against North Vietnamese gunboats in the Gulf of Tonkin on August 5, 1964. These were the first combat missions flown using the F-4B.

MCDONNELL DOUGLAS RF-4B PHANTOM II ▽

McDonnell Douglas RF-4B Phantom II, RM-17, VMCJ-1, Da Nang air base, Vietnam, 1968.
VMCJ-1 Golden Eagles flew photo reconnaissance missions over Vietnam from 1966 until 1970.

MCDONNELL DOUGLAS F-4J PHANTOM II ▽

McDonnell Douglas F-4J Phantom II, DW-7, VMFA-251, MCAS Beaufort, South Carolina, 1974.
VMFA-251 was equipped with F-4s for over 20 years – upgrading to new variants as they became available.

MCDONNELL DOUGLAS F-4N PHANTOM II ▽

McDonnell Douglas F-4N Phantom II, SH-17, VMFAT-101, MCAS El Toro, California, 1975.
VMFAT-101 began training F-4 crews in February 1969 and would continue to do so until it switched to the F/A-18 Hornet in 1987.

VMCJ-1

3091

RM

MARINES

VMFA-251

3888

DW

7

F-4J
153888

MARINES

VMFAT-101

3915

SH

17

F-4N
153915

MARINES

MCDONNELL DOUGLAS F-4N PHANTOM II ▽

McDonnell Douglas F-4N Phantom II, NK-104, VMFA-323, USS *Coral Sea* (CV-43) 1980.
Phantoms of VMFA-323 were due to take part in Operation Eagle Claw, a mission to rescue 52 American staff from the US embassy in Iran on April 24, 1980, which was aborted before it began. This aircraft is seen with recognition markings painted on the outer wings. These were needed to distinguish US support aircraft from F-4s purchased by Iran in the time of the Shah.

Lt (jg) Terrence M Murphy and Ensign Ronald J Fegan of VF-96, flying from USS *Ranger* with call-sign 'Showtime 602', shot down a Chinese MiG-17 on April 9, 1965, for the Phantom's first 'kill'. The first North Vietnamese MiG kills of the war was claimed by Cdr Louis Page and Lt John C Smith of VF-21 'Freelancers', also flying an F-4B, on June 17, 1965.

McDonnell built a total of 649 F-4Bs and they equipped numerous Marine Corps units. VMFA-531 'Grey Ghosts' were assigned to Da Nang air base on April 11, 1965, and their first missions were to provide air cover for Marines on the ground. However, they were

soon flying close air support and before long were joined by VMFA-314 'Black Knights', VMFA-232 'Red Devils', VMFA-323 'Death Rattlers' and VMFA-542 'Bengals' – all flying F-4Bs.

F-4J
While the first Marine Corps F-4Bs were on their way to Vietnam, McDonnell was already working on the next Navy version – the F-4J. It would be powered by new engines, a pair of J79-GE-10s with 17,844lb of thrust each using afterburner, and the new Westinghouse AN/APG-59 pulse doppler radar with AN/AWG-10 Fire Control System was installed in its nose.

This provided look-down, shoot-down capability, with the ability to identify and track low-flying targets.

The crew sat on new Martin-Baker zero-zero ejection seats and the pilot received information from the FCS directly through a helmet-mounted sight. Bigger undercarriage mainwheels were fitted and internal fuel tank capacity was increased.

Another addition was a tailplane with a slotted edge and landing was made easier with a new system in the wings to droop the ailerons by 16.5-degrees when the flaps were lowered, providing more lift at low speed. Automatic flaps were also fitted.

▼ MCDONNELL DOUGLAS F-4B PHANTOM II

McDonnell Douglas F-4B Phantom II, AA-207, VMFA-531, HMS
***Ark Royal*, 1973.**
While operating from the British carrier HMS *Ark Royal* in early 1973,
this USMC Phantom was painted with 892 Naval Air Squadron markings
on its fin.

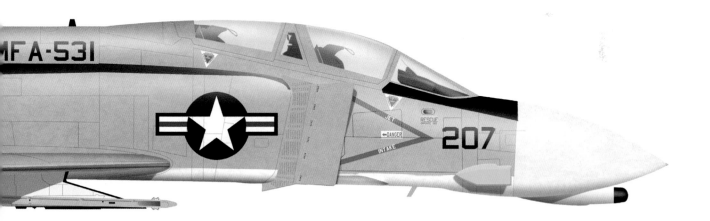

Three F-4Bs were modified to become YF-4J prototypes and the first of them made its maiden flight on June 4, 1965. Testing then commenced and the first full production model F-4J flew for the first time on May 27, 1966. Between the completion of this first example and delivery of the last one in January 1972, a total of 522 were made.

The first Marine Corps unit to receive the F-4J was VMFA-334 in June 1967 and it would later also be flown by VMFA-112, VMFA-115, VMFA-122, VMFA-212, VMFA-232, VMFA-235, VMFA-312, VMFA-333, VMFA-451 and VMFAT-101.

RF-4B
In addition to the F-4B and F-4J, the Marine Corps would also fly a reconnaissance variant, the RF-4B, in Vietnam.

Having been planned by McDonnell from very early in the Phantom's development as the Model 98P, nine RF-4Bs were initially ordered specifically for the Marines in February 1963, with another 37 being added to the order later. The type was unarmed and had the standard aircraft's nose replaced with a camera nose that was 4ft 8.875in longer. This housed three separate bays; the first could accommodate a single forward

oblique or vertical KS-87 camera, the second was fitted with a low-altitude KS-87 and the third had either a single KA-55A or KA-91 high-altitude panoramic camera. Alternatively, the bigger KS-91 or KS-127A cameras could be carried.

With no room for the usual AN/APQ-72 radar, the RF-4B was fitted with the smaller AN/APQ-99 forward-looking J-band monopulse radar with terrain avoidance and terrain following capabilities.

Within the rear cockpit, the reconnaissance systems officer had no flight controls. Two ALE-29A/B chaff/flare dispensers were added, as well as a set of photoflash cartridges for night-time

MCDONNELL DOUGLAS F-4S PHANTOM II ▽

McDonnell Douglas F-4S Phantom II, WD-13, VMFA-212, MCAS Kaneohe Bay, Hawaii, 1983.
This VMFA-212 Phantom displays a mixture of high and low-visibility colours and markings

▼ MCDONNELL DOUGLAS F-4S PHANTOM II

McDonnell Douglas F-4S Phantom II, DR-07, VMFA-312, MCAS Beaufort, South Carolina, 1986.
The F-4S was a modernised F-4J with smokeless engines, wing slats and airframe improvements. VMFA-312 would be the first USMC squadron to receive this variant.

▼ MCDONNELL DOUGLAS F-4S PHANTOM II

McDonnell-Douglas F-4S Phantom II, MG-000, VMFA-321, MAG-41 Detachment A, 1991.
To mark the phasing out of the F-4 from USMC service, this F-4 from VMFA-321 was given a 'Phabulous' colour scheme!

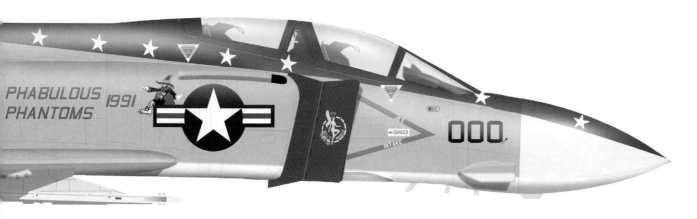

MCDONNELL DOUGLAS RF-4B PHANTOM II ▼

McDonnell Douglas RF-4B Phantom II, RF-36, VMFP-3, MCAS El Toro,
California, 1987.
RF-4Bs were equipped with several cameras installed in a revised nose.
VMFP-3 was created by combining all remaining USMC RF-4B aircraft into
one unit. This example had a striking all-black scheme.

MCDONNELL DOUGLAS F-4S PHANTOM II ▼

McDonnell Douglas F-4S Phantom II, MA-14, VMFA-112, NAS Dallas,
Texas, 1992.
VMFA-112 was a Marine Corps Reserve squadron and the last one to fly
the F-4, outside of test units.

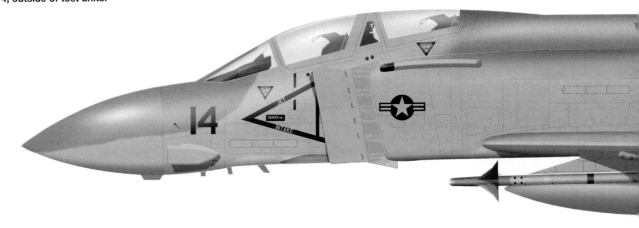

photography. In addition, an AN/APQ-102 SLAR, with its antenna in fairings on the lower fuselage sides, was also installed. An ALQ-126 electronic countermeasures package meant external jammer pods were unnecessary.

While the first 34 RF-4Bs were built on the basic F-4B airframe, the remaining 12 had the modified wing and bigger wheels of the F-4J. Of those 12, the final three had an undernose bulge similar to that of the USAF's RF-4C.

The first RF-4B flew on March 12, 1965, and the Marine Corps received all 46 between May 1965 and December 1970.

VMCJ-3, stationed at Iwakuni in Japan, was first to receive the RF-4B, followed by VMCJ-2 based at MCAS Cherry Point and VMCJ-1, also based at Iwakuni.

The latter flew the first photo reconnaissance mission with the RF-4B on November 3, 1966, from Da Nang and continued to operate from there until 1970, suffering no losses. During this

time the unit would receive aircraft from both VMCJ-2 and VMCJ-3. In 1975, after the war, VMFP-3 was formed at MCAS El Toro to consolidate all remaining Marine Corps RF-4Bs in a single unit. VMFP-3, known as The Eyes of the Corps, would continue to serve with RF-4Bs until its disestablishment in August 1990.

VIETNAM

The first Marine pilot to score a kill in Vietnam was Captain Doyle D Baker, flying a USAF F-4D with Air Force 1st Lt John D Ryan as his weapons systems operator. Baker was on an exchange duty with the Air Force's 13th Tactical Fighter Squadron when he shot down a MiG-17 on December 17, 1967.

More than four and a half years later, on August 12, 1972, Marine Captain Lawrence G Richard was flying a USAF F-4E, also on exchange duty, with Navy Lt Cmdr Michael J Ettel as his weapons systems operator, when he shot down

a MiG-21 with a radar-guided AIM-7E-2 Sparrow missile.

With the war drawing to an end, there would be only one all-Marines MiG kill of the war. Major Lee T 'Bear' Lasseter and Captain 'Lil' John D Cummings of VMFA-333 'Fighting Shamrocks', flying an F-4J off USS *America*, shot down a MiG-21 using a Sidewinder on September 11, 1972. The pair then damaged a second MiG with their last missile.

A total of 72 Marine F-4Bs would be lost in combat during the Vietnam War – 65 shot down by anti-aircraft fire, six blown up on the ground by enemy forces and one shot down by a MiG. Another 23 Phantoms were written off in accidents.

While most Marine Phantoms were employed primarily in the close air support role, Marine Phantoms were also involved in Operation Rolling Thunder during 1968 and in Operation Linebacker during April 1972. Marine F-4Js would be the last American aircraft operating

in South East Asia, with VMFA-232 eventually departing from Nam Phong air base in Thailand in August 1973.

THE F-4N AND S
Even as Marine Phantoms were engaging in heavy combat over Vietnam, back home the Blue Angels demonstration team converted to F-4Js on December 23, 1968. The team's seven aircraft had their AWG-10 weapons control systems replaced with ballast to maintain their centre of gravity and their variable intake ramps were disabled since they would only be flying at subsonic speeds. Four dummy Sparrow missiles were installed below the fuselage – with the forward pair containing red and blue dye while the pair at the rear held oil for creating smoke.

The Blue Angels F-4Js' fuel tanks were modified so they could fly inverted for more than 30 seconds. Their cockpits were also changed, with the weapons selector removed and switches added

for the smoke and dye systems. The automatic flaps system was removed as well and the aircraft were retrofitted with older J79-GE-8 engines.

After the F-4J was brought into service, Project Bee Line was begun to bring 228 surviving F-4Bs up to a similar standard. This involved the addition of the AN/ASW-25 datalink, ECM equipment and the F-4J's helmet-mounted sight. Sidewinder Expanded Acquisition Mode (SEAM), IFF, and a dogfight computer were also fitted. The old J79-GE-8 engines swapped for a new smokeless version of the J79-GE-10 and the airframes underwent structural strengthening. The aerodynamic improvements implemented in the F-4J, such as the slotted tailplanes, were added too. The 228 Bee Line aircraft received the new designation F-4N and the first example flew on June 4, 1972. F-4Ns would be flown by VFMA-112, VFMA-134, VFMA-314, VFMA-321, VFMA-323, VFMA-351, VFMA-531 and VMFAT-101.

A total of 265 surviving F-4Js underwent their own similar programme beginning in June 1975. Their airframes were strengthened, wiring looms were replaced, and wings were modified with leading edge slats for better manoeuvrability. The new AN/AWG-10B FCS was fitted and radios were upgraded. Improvements were made to the avionics cooling vents and the old J79-GE-10s were replaced with the new smokeless version. These aircraft were designated F-4S and would be flown by VFMA-111, VFMA-112, VFMA-115, VFMA-134, VFMA-212, VFMA-232, VFMA-235, VFMA-251, VFMA-312, VFMA-321, VFMA-333, VFMA-451 and VMFAT-101.

During the early 1980s, Marine F-4 squadrons began transitioning to the F/A-18. The last Marine Corps Phantom was an F-4S operated by VMFA-112 'Cowboys' at NAS Dallas, Texas. It was retired on January 18, 1992.

HAWKER SIDDELEY AV-8A HARRIER

The British Harrier, with its ability to operate without a runway, hover like a helicopter and provide highly accurate close support, was well suited to service with the USMC.

HAWKER SIDDELEY AV-8A HARRIER ▽

Hawker Siddeley AV-8A Harrier, Hawker Siddeley Dunsfold factory, UK, 1971.
The USMC's first Hawker Siddeley Harriers entered service in 1971 under the designation AV-8A. One of the earliest examples is seen here as it appeared at the handover ceremony.

HAWKER SIDDELEY AV-8A HARRIER ▽

Hawker Siddeley AV-8A Harrier, WF-2, VMA-513 Detachment A, MCAS Cherry Point, North Carolina, 1975.
This VMA-513 Detachment A Harrier carries a combination of bombs, rockets and gun pod for short-range ground-attack, a role well suited to USMC operations.

1971-1987

Development of the Hawker P.1127 commenced in 1957, based on the Bristol Engine Company's Pegasus vectored thrust engine. The aircraft had a single Pegasus, mounted centrally within the fuselage, providing 13,000lb-ft of thrust through four nozzles – two on either size.

The nozzles could be pointed downwards to enable vertical take-off before being rotated to point rearwards for subsonic horizontal flight. Thrust control was such that the aircraft could hover in one spot or move slowly in any direction while remaining pointed at a fixed location.

The P.1127 had short wings, swept tail surfaces and a short pointed nose ahead of the single-seat cockpit. The undercarriage was unusual – consisting of a single nosewheel, a double wheel strut directly beneath the fuselage and

one smaller wheel extending beneath the tip of each wing to provide four points of contact with the ground.

The early development of the P.1127 took place during a period of deep defence spending cuts in Britain and Hawker financed the project from its own pocket. However, there was American interest even at this early stage and NASA was able to provide research assistance, conducting wind tunnel tests at its Langley Research Center in support of the programme.

The first prototype P.1127, XP831, was delivered to Dunsfold Aerodrome in Surrey for static engine testing on July 15, 1960, and the first untethered free flight hover was achieved just over four months later on November 19. The aircraft's first conventional flight was on February 13, 1961. Testing progressed steadily, with five further P.1127s being constructed.

In 1962, the British government approached the US and West Germany for a financial contribution towards the nine production-standard aircraft for evaluation. An agreement was reached and Hawker received a formal Instruction to Proceed on May 22, 1962.

The result was the improved Kestrel FGA.1, the first example of which made its flight debut on March 7, 1964. An evaluation squadron consisting of British, American and West German pilots was established at RAF West Raynham in the UK on October 15, 1964, and testing commenced. One aircraft was lost during this time and six of the eight survivors were then transferred to the US for evaluation by the US Army, Air Force and Navy under the designation XV-6A Kestrel.

When this evaluation came to the end, four were passed to the USAF

HAWKER SIDDELEY TAV-8A HARRIER ▽

Hawker Siddeley TAV-8A Harrier, KD-04, VMAT-203, MCAS Cherry Point, North Carolina, 1978.
The special flying characteristics of the Harrier called for a dedicated two-seat training variant – supplied by Hawker Siddeley in the form of the TAV-8A.

HAWKER SIDDELEY AV-8A HARRIER

Hawker Siddeley AV-8A Harrier, NM-606, VMA-231, USS *Franklin D. Roosevelt* (CV-42), 1976.
Harriers of VMA-231 were deployed aboard the USS *Franklin D. Roosevelt* a couple of years before its decommissioning and were equipped with fixed in-flight refuelling probes.

HAWKER SIDDELEY AV-8A HARRIER

Hawker Siddeley AV-8A Harrier, WH-16, VMA-542, MCAS Beaufort, South Carolina, 1978.
Deactivated in 1970 following its return from Vietnam, VMFA-542 was reinstated in January 1972 as VMA-542 and equipped with the AV-8A.

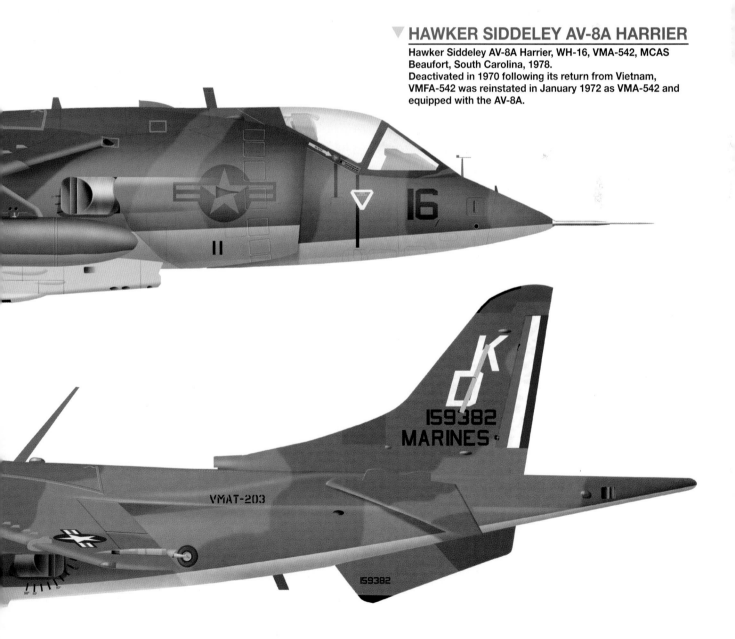

while two went to NASA. No orders were forthcoming however – none of the three services involved in the trials felt that the Kestrel in its then-current form was sufficiently capable to justify a purchase.

Nevertheless, the RAF decided to buy 60 examples of a fully improved Kestrel as the Harrier GR.1 in early 1967. The first of these made its flight debut on December 28, 1967. The type then officially entered RAF service on April 1, 1969. Rather than being an upgraded Kestrel, the Harrier was a completely new aircraft. Its wing was the result of a complete redesign, its undercarriage was strengthened and it featured two under-fuselage weapons pod attachment points plus four underwing

pylons. These could accommodate up to 5300lb of stores ranging from rocket pods to iron bombs, drop tanks and air-to-air missiles for self-defence.

Inside the cockpit, a Martin-Baker Mk.9 zero-zero ejection seat was installed. It had no radar, however, being fitted instead with a Ferranti FE541 inertial navigation and attack system.

Meanwhile, the USMC had become interested in the type's potential, Marine pilots having test-flown the Kestrel during early 1968 and given it strongly positive reviews. Two more USMC pilots went to the Farnborough Airshow later that year to fly the Harrier and were similarly enthusiastic. Consequently, in early 1969, the US placed an order for an even dozen

aircraft – despite opposition from those who disliked the idea of buying a foreign aircraft. Funding for the procurement was formally approved on September 20, 1969 – again, despite strong opposition – and the contract was signed on December 23 of the same year.

McDonnell Douglas secured a 15-year contract to build the type under licence in St Louis with the US designation being AV-8A. However, defence budget limitations made it uneconomical to set up a full manufacturing production line. Instead, all of the USMC's AV-8As were built at Hawker Siddeley's factory in Kingston UK before being disassembled, shipped to the US, then reassembled by McDonnell Douglas.

HAWKER SIDDELEY AV-8C HARRIER ▼

Hawker Siddeley AV-8C Harrier, 621, Patuxent River, Maryland, 1981. Before the delivery of the new AV-8B, it was decided to upgrade some AV-8As to C standard. This new variant featured lift improvement devices such as new ventral strakes on the fuselage or the gun pods, radar warning antennas and improvements to communications, weapons and other systems.

The first AV-8A was the 62nd Harrier off the production line and it first flew on November 20, 1970. Initially, the type was powered by a Pegasus 10 engine but from the 11th example this was changed to the Pegasus 11 – which was then retrofitted to the first 10 aircraft.

Less than a year later, the AV-8As had their FE541 nav-attack systems stripped out and replaced with US-developed systems. Their Martin-Baker ejection seats were also removed and replaced with the Stencel SEU-3/A model. It was thought at the time that this seat would also be used for the Grumman F-14 Tomcat and McDonnell Douglas F/A-18 Hornet – resulting in commonality between all three aircraft. However, neither the F-14 nor the F/A-18 ended up with the Stencel unit but the AV-8A was by then forced to retain it.

The first AV-8A unit was VMA-513, stationed at Yuma in Arizona, which received its first aircraft in 1971. VMA-231 and VMA-542 followed while VMAT-203 provided conversion training. This latter role proved to be an essential because the Harrier had unique characteristics which meant neither conventional jet nor helicopter pilots could fly it well without extensive retraining. A two-seat trainer variant was therefore acquired with the designation TAV-8A.

VMA-513's first deployment with the Harrier was aboard USS *Guam*, which had been converted into an Interim Sea Control Ship intended to supplement the US Navy's carriers with a mix of Harriers and helicopters. The concept was trialled from 1971 to 1973 and was followed by further exercises intended to assess the Harrier's

suitability for various other types of vessel – including amphibious assault ships and conventional aircraft carriers. To this end, 14 AV-8As of VMA-231 were deployed aboard USS *Franklin D. Roosevelt* for six months starting in June 1976.

All these trials and tests served to demonstrate that the Harrier could operate in weather conditions out at sea that would render conventional carrier jets unusable – although they also demonstrated the type's unique ability to damage painted non-skid surfaces on the *FDR's* flight deck with their concentrated hot exhaust down-blast.

Land-based exercises also proved the Harrier's worth: since a runway was unnecessary, Harrier forward bases could be established in under 24 hours in almost any location 20 miles from the edge of a given battlefield while more

▼ HAWKER SIDDELEY AV-8A HARRIER

Hawker Siddeley AV-8A Harrier, CG-00, VMA-231, NAS Fallon, Nevada, 1983.
During deployment to NAS Fallon, a Harrier was seen painted with white areas over the usual camouflage scheme; it carries MK.77 incendiary bombs.

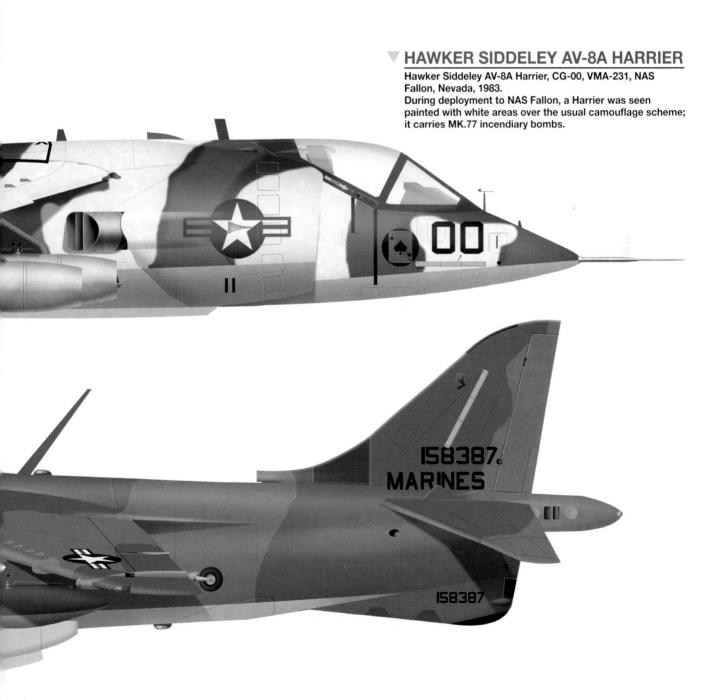

permanent bases were established 50 miles back from the front. These short distances meant more sorties could be flown during a given time period and fuel consumption would be significantly reduced compared to jet aircraft operating from a runway.

Similarly, Harrier forward bases could be concealed with relative ease and moved elsewhere at short notice.

The USMC would eventually order 102 AV-8As and eight TAV-8As. By the mid-1970s, the service was already planning to acquire a dramatically

improved version of the Harrier under the designation AV-8B – for which McDonnell Douglas would finally be able to set up a full production line – but as an interim measure decided to implement some of its features in a modification to the AV-8A known as the AV-8C.

HAWKER SIDDELEY AV-8A HARRIER ▽

Hawker Siddeley AV-8A Harrier, WF-17, VMA-513, USS *Guadalcanal* (LPH 7), 1983.
VMA-513 was the first USMC squadron to operate the AV-8A, being deployed both to land bases and aboard amphibious assault ships. AV-8As could carry the larger 300 US gallon external fuel tanks in place of the more commonly used 120 US gallon tanks.

HAWKER SIDDELEY AV-8A HARRIER ▽

Hawker Siddeley AV-8A, WH-25, VMA-542, MCAS Cherry Point, North Carolina, 1978.
Although tasked mainly with air-to-ground missions, the Harriers could still perform the air-to-air role, relying on its agility, missiles and gun. This aircraft displays markings attesting to its air-to-air capacity during training.

HAWKER SIDDELEY AV-8A HARRIER ▽

Hawker Siddeley AV-8A, KD-11, VMAT-203, MCAS Cherry Point, North Carolina, 1980.
VMAT-203, the USMC AV-8 training squadron, used both twin- and single-seat variants of the aircraft.

Between 1979 and 1984 a total of 47 AV-8As were upgraded to become AV-8Cs (the original plan had called for 60 AV-8Cs – but the conversion work was only carried out on 47), with structural strengthening, an onboard oxygen generation system, lift improvement devices (large fixed longitudinal ventral fuselage strakes and a retractable cross-dam behind the nose-gear), a Litton AN/ALR-45F radar warning receiver and an AN/ALE-39 chaff/flare dispenser. The first AV-8C flew on May 5, 1979.

During their time in service, some 40 AV-8As and Cs were lost in accidents with around 30 pilots killed. The Marine Corps commenced a programme of retirement for the surviving aircraft in March 1985 with the last examples being taken out of service in 1987.

MCDONNELL DOUGLAS F/A-18A-D

Since its early days as a cheap lightweight fighter, the original F/A-18 has grown and evolved to become a capable and reliable all-rounder. The US Navy may have retired the so-called 'legacy' type but it remains on the front line with the Marines.

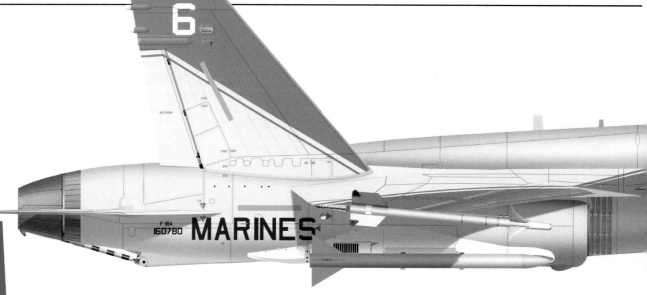

1984–PRESENT

MCDONNELL DOUGLAS/BOEING F/A-18A HORNET ▽

McDonnell Douglas/Boeing F/A-18A Hornet, SH-12, VMFAT-101, MCAS Miramar, California, 2007.
VMFAT-101 has provided training for Hornet crews since 1987 – 34 years and counting at the time of writing – as the dedicated F/A-18 Fleet Replacement Squadron of the USMC.

he Marine Corps is steadily transitioning from the Hornets and Harriers of decades past to the new F-35B and C – but the 'classic' 1980s-era F/A-18A-Ds aren't done yet, not by a long shot.

The aircraft's story begins not with McDonnell Douglas but with rival manufacturer Northrop all the way back in 1952. As other companies were making ever larger, heavier, faster fighters, Northrop hit upon the concept of something lighter and more manoeuvrable but still supersonic – which became the F-5.

This was such a success in terms of international sales that the company decided to try for a repeat performance during the mid-1960s. Basic concepts for a more modern light fighter based on the F-5 template were drawn up in 1966 and extensive wind tunnel testing and aerodynamic refinement resulted in the polished final design which emerged in 1970.

The new aircraft retained the F-5's character but with substantial Leading Edge Root eXtensions (LERX) added to its wings for better handling at high angles of attack and two tailfins rather than the original one, for improved manoeuvrability and enhanced stability.

The 1971 Paris Air Show – a great showcase for international customers – saw Northrop displaying a full-scale mock-up of its P-530 design, also known as the 'Cobra' because the LERX gave it a somewhat 'hooded' look. Both single- and twin-engine options for a full production version were offered as the P-610 (single) and P-600 (twin).

A year later, Northrop entered the P-600 for the USAF's lightweight fighter (LWF) competition against rival designs from Boeing, General Dynamics and LTV. Prototypes of both the GD and Northrop designs were ordered and a fly-off ensued between the YF-16 and YF-17 – the latter being the P-600's official designation. Much to Northrop's dismay,

the YF-16 was eventually picked by the Air Force to become the famous F-16 and the YF-17 was passed over.

Yet all was not lost because the US Navy was also looking for a light multirole fighter to complement its heavy F-14 fleet defence interceptor and replace its ageing A-7s and F-4s in the strike-fighter role. The subsequent Navy ACF or NACF competition saw GD and LTV team up to create a navalised YF-16, while McDonnell Douglas lent its carrier fighter design expertise to Northrop for a navalised YF-17.

It is unsurprising, in retrospect, that the twin-engine YF-17 defeated the single-engine YF-16 in May 1975 and it was decided that what had been the 'Cobra' would become the F-18. And so, with an eye on those international sales, Northrop signed a deal where McDonnell Douglas would build the Navy's F-18 while it would keep what it assumed would be the more profitable F-18L – the land-based version.

▼ MCDONNELL DOUGLAS F/A-18 HORNET

McDonnell Douglas F/A-18A Hornet, 6, NAS Patuxent River, Maryland, 1981.
The F/A-18 prototype and Full Scale Development aircraft all displayed Marines markings on the right aft fuselage with correspondent Navy titles on the other side. FSD aircraft 6 was used for spin testing.

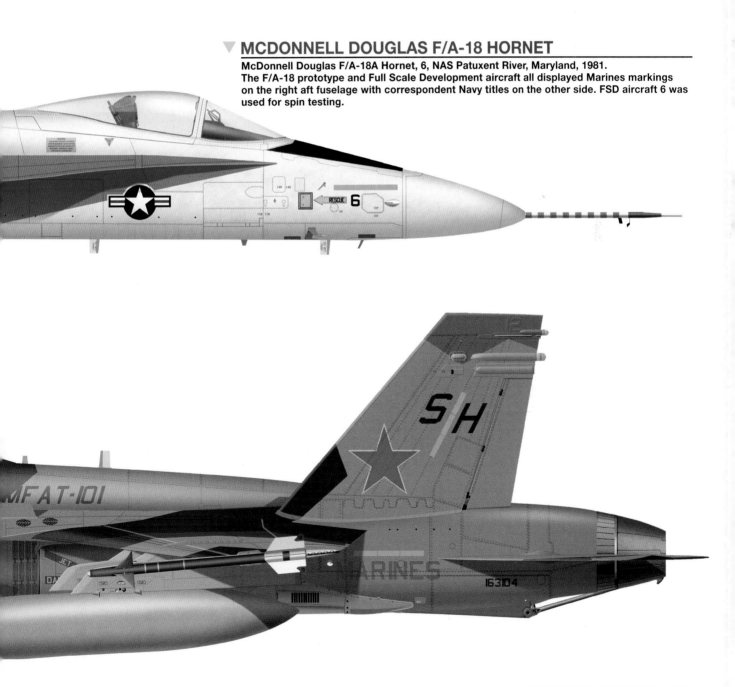

Sadly for Northrop, international customers flocked to the F-16 and the F-18L found no takers. The aircraft it had spent decades fine-tuning was now in the hands of McDonnell Douglas! The Navy ordered 11 F-18s – a pair of two-seaters and nine single seaters – for evaluation and McDonnell Douglas duly set about converting the YF-17 design for carrier operations.

This involved the installation of a more powerful development of the YJ101 engine used for the YF-17 (General Electric's F404), bigger wings that could fold, high-lift devices, beefed up landing gear, greater internal fuel capacity and in-flight refuelling gear. The first F-18

prototype flew on November 18, 1978 and the last of the 11 was received by the Navy in March 1980. These were assigned to Fleet Replacement Squadron VFA-125 for training crews. Testing and evaluation then lasted until October 1982, by which time the type had been redesignated F/A-18 to indicate its multirole capability.

The production model Hornet was 50% aluminium, 17% steel, 13% titanium and 10% glass reinforced plastic. It was powered by two F404-GE-400s, each providing 16,000lb-ft of thrust with afterburner, with D-shaped intakes and splitter plates. Its wings were about 14% larger than those of the YF-17 and featured a power-folding mechanism.

The Hornet also had a strong undercarriage with two wheels on the nose and a catapult attachment included. An arresting hook was installed at the aircraft's rear.

The pilot sat below a full-vision canopy on a Martin-Baker Mark 10 ejection seat, facing three multifunction displays linked to the aircraft's Hughes AN/APG-65 radar, which could be toggled between navigation, air combat and strike modes. There was also an AN/ALQ-126B jamming system, AN/ALE-39 chaff and flare dispensers and an AN/ALR-50 radar warning system, plus the usual radio, IFF and navigation beacon.

MCDONNELL DOUGLAS F/A-18A HORNET ▼

McDonnell Douglas F/A-18A Hornet, AK-103, VMFA-451, USS Coral Sea (CV-43), 1989.
VMFA-451 received the new Hornet in 1987 and deployed aboard USS Coral Sea in 1989. The squadron would participate in Operation Desert Shield and subsequently in Desert Storm, operating from land bases.

MCDONNELL DOUGLAS F/A-18 HORNET

McDonnell Douglas F/A-18A Hornet, VW-03, VMFA-314, MCAS El Toro, California, 1983
VMFA-314 was the first USMC operational squadron to be equipped with the new F/A-18 Hornet in 1983. It participated in air strikes against Libya on April 15, 1986, during Operation El Dorado Canyon – in retaliation for a Berlin discotheque bombing ten days earlier which killed three people and injured 229. Two of the dead and 79 of the injured were Americans.

A single M61A1 Vulcan 20mm cannon was mounted centrally in the top of the nose in a position which shielded the pilot from muzzle flash – preventing night blindness – and allowed gases from the weapon to pass over the LERX without entering the engine intakes. Each wingtip had a single Sidewinder launch rail and there were two pylons for external stores beneath each wing. A single Sparrow-type missile could also be recessed into the fuselage on either side and there was a centreline fuselage hardpoint as well.

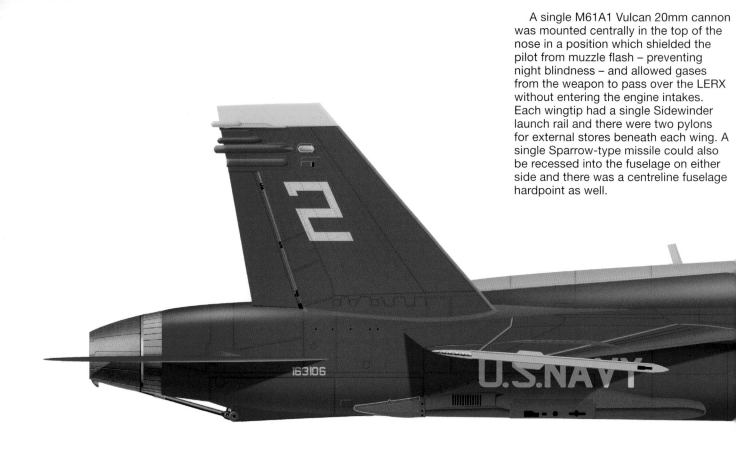

▼ MCDONNELL DOUGLAS/BOEING F/A-18D HORNET

McDonnell Douglas/ Boeing F/A-18D Hornet, EA-14, VMFA(AW)-332, MCAS Beaufort, South Carolina, 2005.
Some F/A-18Ds were fitted with the Advanced Tactical Airborne Reconnaissance System (ATARS) in a modified nose, providing multi-sensor data gathering and transmission capability. These aircraft are integrated into squadrons with unmodified F/A-18Ds.

A huge range of external stores could be carried up to 15,500lb – including Zuni rocket pods, AGM-88 HARM anti-radar missiles, AGM-65 Maverick air-to-surface missiles, AN/AAS-38 Nite Hawk targeting pods, jamming pods, 1250 litre external fuel tanks and much more. Using external tanks and the buddy system, an F/A-18A could even operate as a tanker too. McDonnell Douglas made 371 F/A-18As between 1980 and 1987.

The Marine Corps introduced the F/A-18A into service on January 7, 1983, with VMFA-314 at MCAS El Toro.

F/A-18B/C/D
The combat-capable F/A-18B trainer had a second cockpit with dual controls but was otherwise nearly identical to the F/A-18A – the extra cockpit requiring the sacrifice of about 6% of internal fuel capacity and the reshuffling of some electronics. Forty were built.

There were efforts to create a reconnaissance variant by fitting a camera nose to an F/A-18B, and a modified example flew on August 15, 1984, but there was no production order. However, the USMC would later order F/A-18Ds with nose-mounted reconnaissance packages.

McDonnell Douglas replaced the F/A-18A/B on the production line with the single seat F/A-18C and two-seater F/A-18D in 1987. Little changed externally except for a new strake being added to the rear of the LERX – and this was retrofitted to all F/A-18As and Bs so it was difficult to tell older and newer aircraft apart.

Inside though, the F/A-18Cs and Ds had improved Martin-Baker Mark 15 ejection seats and electronics upgrades which allowed them to carry newer versions of the Maverick, the AIM-120 AMRAAM, and the latest Sparrow. They also got the new AN/ALR-67 radar, AN/ALE-47 chaff and flare dispensers, more modern computer systems and an upgraded air flow system to keep them cool. The F/A-18C prototype – a modified F/A-18A – first flew on September 3, 1986.

▲ MCDONNELL DOUGLAS/BOEING F/A-18C HORNET

McDonnell Douglas/Boeing F/A-18C Hornet, 2, Blue Angels, NAS Pensacola, Florida, 2017.
The Blue Angels team includes both US Navy and USMC aviators, with at least one of the F/A-18s being piloted by a Marines officer.

MCDONNELL DOUGLAS/BOEING F/A-18B HORNET ▽

McDonnell Douglas/Boeing F/A-18B Hornet, NJ-400, VFA-125, NAS Lemoore,
California, 2010.
VFA-125 uses aircraft and personnel from the USMC and US Navy to provide training
for F/A-18 crews for both services and even foreign Hornet operators. Some of its
aircraft feature particularly striking colour schemes such as this one.

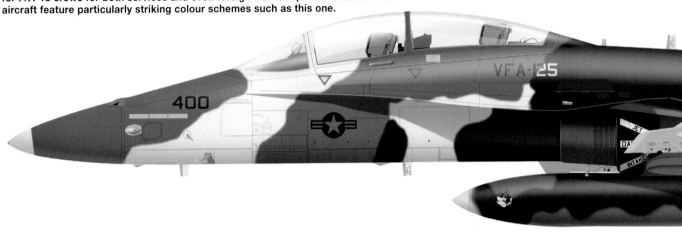

MCDONNELL DOUGLAS/BOEING F/A-18A HORNET ▽

McDonnell Douglas/ Boeing F/A-18A Hornet, AB-201, VMFA-312, USS *Enterprise*
(CVN-65), 2004.
VMFA-312 Checkerboards deployed aboard USS *Enterprise* during 2003-2004 in
support of Operation Iraqi Freedom. One of their Hornets displayed this unique
splinter camouflage.

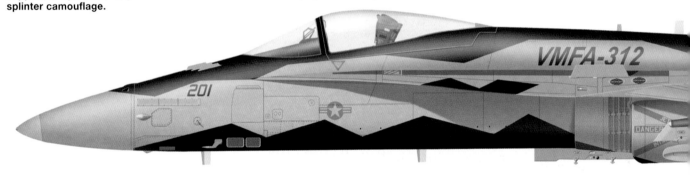

MCDONNELL DOUGLAS/BOEING F/A-18D HORNET

McDonnell Douglas/ Boeing F/A-18D Hornet, VK-04, VMFA(AW)-121, MCAS Miramar, California, 2002.
The USMC uses the F/A-18D as a dedicated attack platform, equipping several squadrons with it. VMFA(AW)-121 became the first such squadron in 1989, subsequently participating in Operation Desert Storm.

AGEING FLEET

Just three years later, McDonnell Douglas moved to production of the F/A-18C+ and D+, adding night vision goggle compatibility and a digital moving map. November 1, 1989 saw the first F/A-18C+ delivered and from 1991 the aircraft could also carry the AN/AAS-38A laser targeting pod, followed by the AN/AAS-38B pod with auto-tracking in 1996.

In 1992 the fleet was re-engined with the more reliable F404-GE-402, developing 17,600lb-ft of thrust with afterburner, and two years later the aircraft were fitted with the new AN/APG-73 multimode radar with increased range. A GPS receiver was installed in 1995 and thereafter radar absorbing material was added to provide a degree of stealth capability.

A total of 466 F/A-18Cs and 161 F/A-18Ds were built for the Marine Corps and USN. Including export models, a grand total of 1480 F/A-18A/B/C/D variants were built. Another wave of upgrades to F/A-18s with sufficiently low flight hours commenced in 2000, bringing with it modifications to support the latest AMRAAM.

As time wore on, however, the Marines' Hornets became increasingly difficult to maintain. In 2015, it was reported that one in five was grounded for lengthy maintenance. By the following year, 41% of all Marine aircraft were grounded due to ongoing maintenance and repair difficulties. In fact, the Hornet accounted for a large proportion of this figure – with just 72 out of 280 capable of flight by the end of 2016.

The Navy began retiring its Hornets in 2017 and their last operational deployment was made in 2018. Some 136 aircraft were moved to the Davis-Monthan Air Force Base boneyard in Arizona while examples in a better state were passed to the Marine Corps.

HORNET 'SUNDOWN'

Under the latest plans, the USMC will retain Hornets until 2030, when they will finally be phased out and replaced by F-35s. As such, plans were set out in September 2020 to keep the Marine Corps F/A-18s competitive through a series of updates. A batch of 84 aircraft – those in the best condition and with the greatest number of flying hours remaining – will be fitted with the Raytheon AN/APG-79(v)4 Active Electronically Scanned Array (AESA) radar. This is based on the AN/APG-79(v)1 fitted to the Navy's Block 2/3 F/A-18E/F Super Hornets and EA-18G Growlers. They will also get the ALE-67(v)3 Radar Warning Receiver and the ALQ-214(v)5, which replaces the ALQ-165 Airborne Self-Protection Jammer.

The F/A-18 was originally designed for 6000 flying hours, which was then extended to 8000 hours then finally 10,000 hours. It is planned that all remaining F/A-18As and Bs will be retired and 11 active squadrons plus one reserve will be reduced to seven composite squadrons with seven Lot 15 and above F/A-18Cs and five Lot

MCDONNELL DOUGLAS/BOEING F/A-18C HORNET ▼

McDonnell Douglas/ Boeing F/A-18C Hornet, WT-01, VMFA-232, Al-Jaber air base, Kuwait, 2003.
Starting on March 3, 2003, VMFA-232 Red Devils flew close and deep air support for advancing infantry columns during Operation Iraqi Freedom – providing 24-hour a day cover as Marines fought through Nasiriyah and Baghdad.

MCDONNELL DOUGLAS/BOEING F/A-18C HORNET

McDonnell Douglas/Boeing F/A-18C Hornet, WS-401, VMFA-323, MCAS Miramar, California, 2019.
The F/A-18 has a tremendous weapons carriage capability. Although not operationally common, this VMFA-323 F/A-18C has the type's maximum loadout of 10 AIM-120 AMRAAM Slammer air-to-air missiles plus two Sidewinders.

MCDONNELL DOUGLAS F/A-18A HORNET

McDonnell Douglas F/A-18A Hornet, MF-00, VMFA-134, NAS Miramar, California, 1994.
Like other USMC aircraft, F/A-18s use the probe and drogue refuelling system, being equipped with a retractable probe. VMFA-314 is a reserve squadron that flew Hornets until 2008. This aircraft has a false canopy painted on the lower front fuselage.

14 and above F/A-18Ds each. These will have each undergone extensive assessment to determine fatigue life with particular attention paid to the wing roots. This area of the aircraft, if it needs repair, requires a time-consuming and expensive structural upgrade known as Center Barrel Replacement Plus. The reserve unit, VMFA-112 'Cowboys' was transitioning from F/A-18A+ aircraft to a fleet of 19 low-hours Lot 10 and 11 F/A-18Cs. Those would be upgraded to C+ configuration.

During 2023-2024 it was planned to give the 84 active service F/A-18Cs and Ds an Automatic Ground Collision Avoidance System plus upgrades to handle the latest weapons – AIM-9X Block II, AIM-120D AMRAAM and AGR-20A Advanced Precision Kill Weapon System – effectively Hydra 70 unguided rockets with a new laser guidance kit which converts them into precision guided munitions.

In March 2021, it was reported that VMFA-323 'Death Rattlers' had returned from a 10-month deployment aboard USS *Nimitz* which marked the final deployment of Marine Corps F/A-18s aboard a carrier. The last flight of an F/A-18C from a carrier deck took place on February 25, 2021. Henceforth, the Marines' Hornets will only operate from land bases.

HORNETS IN ACTION

Marine Corps Hornets have seen action numerous times over the last four decades but perhaps their finest hour – in fact the first large scale combat use of the F/A-18 – was Operation Desert Storm in 1991. Forty-eight F/A-18s and A-6Es of Marine Aircraft Group 11 (MAG 11), loaded with bombs and High-Speed Antiradiation Missiles (HARM), supported by EA-6Bs took off from Shaikh Isa Air Base in Bahrain at 0400 on January 17, 1991. Having refuelled along the way from KC-130s, they flew over Iraq to hit targets including Scud missile launchers and SAM sites. Alongside them were USAF F-4G Wild Weasel Vs and British RAF GR.1 Tornados.

When they reached Iraqi airspace above 25,000ft, they abruptly encountered a barrage of largely unaimed AAA fire as well as surface-to-air missiles. Nevertheless, Marines fired 100 HARMs at Iraqi radars on the first day of Desert Storm alone. As the campaign progressed, the Marines systematically took apart the Iraqi air defence system and repeatedly hit targets in the Marine zone of southern Kuwait.

Enhancing the control of strike aircraft was Marine All-Weather Attack Squadron 121 (VMFA(AW)-121 Green Knights). This squadron of F/A-18D two-seaters operated in the battlefield air-interdiction or deep air support role, controlling air strikes. They located targets using binoculars and night vision goggles, marked them with smoke and provided on-site control of attack aircraft. Their target priority order was artillery and rocket launchers, armour, infantry and

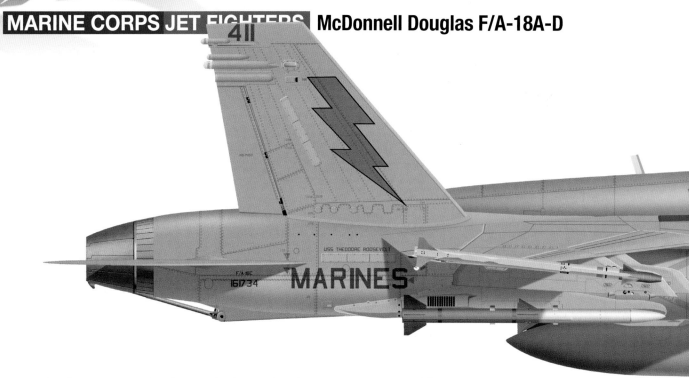

MCDONNELL DOUGLAS/BOEING F/A-18D HORNET ▼

McDonnell Douglas/Boeing F/A-18D Hornet, BT-01, VMFA(AW)-242, MCAS Iwakuni, Japan, 2010.
VMFA(AW)-242 Bats used its F/A-18Ds in support of Operation Iraqi Freedom. It was redesignated VMFA-242 in October 2020 and currently flies F-35Bs from MCAS Iwakuni in Japan.

▼ MCDONNELL DOUGLAS/BOEING F/A-18C HORNET

McDonnell-Douglas/ Boeing F/A-18C Hornet, AB-411, VMFA-251, USS *Theodore Roosevelt* (CVN-71), 2015.
VMFA-251 Thunderbolts made regular carrier deployments alongside similarly-equipped US Navy squadrons prior to its deactivation on April 23, 2020. At the time of writing it was due to be re-activated in 2025 as an F-35C unit stationed at MCAS Cherry Point.

▼ MCDONNELL DOUGLAS F/A-18C HORNET

McDonnell Douglas F/A-18C Hornet, DB-06, VMFA-235, Al Jubail airport, Saudi Arabia, 1991.
One of the VMFA-235's Hornets is seen here configured for ground-attack missions during Operation Desert Storm, when the squadron operated from land bases.

MCDONNELL DOUGLAS/BOEING F/A-18A++ ▼

McDonnell Douglas/Boeing F/A-18A++ Hornet, VF-201, VMFA-115, MCAS Beaufort, South Carolina, 2012.
The F/A-18A++ is an upgrade A+ variant with additional features including a new ejection seat and helmet displays, among others. This VMFA-115 aircraft features particularly patriotic fin art.

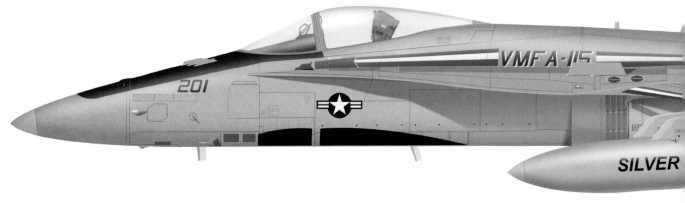

▼ MCDONNELL DOUGLAS/BOEING F/A-18D HORNET

McDonnell Douglas/Boeing F/A-18D Hornet, WK-00, VMFA(AW)-224, MCAS Beaufort, South Carolina, 2005.
This VMFA(AW)-224 Hornet is painted in a very tiger-like colour scheme, reflecting the squadron's emblem.

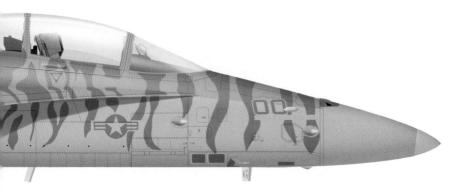

▼ MCDONNELL DOUGLAS/BOEING F/A-18D HORNET

McDonnell Douglas/Boeing F/A-18D Hornet, ED-01, VMFA(AW)-533, MCAS Beaufort, South Carolina, 2019.
VMFA(AW)-533 sometimes deployed its Hornets carrying a total of five external fuel tanks – for operations such as Desert Storm, Southern Watch and Iraqi Freedom – as seen on this aircraft.

lastly trench lines. With support from KC-130s, the F/A-18Ds could remain on station for two 30-minute periods, refuelling in between.

By the third week of the campaign, VMFA(AW)-121 was flying several sorties every night to seek out fresh targets using their enhanced equipment and night vision goggles. Once a target was identified, particularly artillery, it would be passed to a 'wolf pack' of Marine F/A-18s, AH-1s or AV-8Bs to destroy.

As the battle progressed, Marine aviators began assigning their own place names for commonly visited latitude/longitude coordinates – such as 'Ice Cube Tray', the 'Elbow', the 'Crotch', the 'Jacks' and the 'National Forest'. This made navigation easier in what could be largely featureless desert terrain.

Despite suffering heavy casualties early on, the Iraqi air defence system remained a threat throughout the campaign and the Coalition lost 37 fixed-wing aircraft – seven of them operated by the Marines. Not a single Marines F/A-18 was lost however – despite some being hit by gunfire or even caught in the blast of exploding infrared or heat-seeking missiles. The F/A-18's design, with the hot engine exhaust to the extreme rear of the aircraft, made it less vulnerable.

On a number of occasions, Coalition aircraft mistakenly fired on friendly ground forces. For example, on January 29, 1991, a USAF Fairchild Republic A-10 hit a Marine light armoured vehicle with an AGM-65 missile and killed seven Marines. However, no F/A-18s were ever involved in these 'fratricides' – a fact attributed to the improved situational awareness provided by the aircraft's moving map display.

In the early hours of February 26 it was confirmed, by an F/A-18D, that Iraqi forces were retreating from Kuwait – a mass of vehicles moving out of Kuwait City – and it was decided that they should not be allowed to escape. The road from Kuwait City to Safwan, Iraq, became the infamous 'Highway of Death', with thousands of vehicles caught out in the open as they fled. One F/A-18 pilot of VMFA-314 described a typical attack on this route as follows: "Aircraft were darting and diving over the entire area. Sharks at a feeding frenzy… [The F/A-18D] put a mark down on a stretch of road and told me and Toss [his wingman] to work that point and stay east of the highway. They had another two-ship work the same point except that they stayed west of the highway. It was like a dream come true… it was all laid out in front of us. Kids in a candy store."

Desert Storm ended the following day. The F/A-18s had flown more sorties than any other Marine or Navy jet. During the ground war of Desert Storm, Marine aviators across the board flew 2932 Combat Air Support missions, compared to 1361 by the USAF and none by the Navy. The Marines F/A-18s would return to Kuwait 12 years later to provide air support during Operation Iraqi Freedom.

MCDONNELL
DOUGLAS AV-8B HARRIER II

The Harrier II VTOL attack aircraft is more powerful, more adaptable and more capable than its predecessor. It is currently operated by five active operational Marine Corps squadrons plus a Fleet Replacement Squadron and is subject to ongoing upgrades – despite its successor, the F-35, entering service.

MCDONNELL DOUGLAS-BAE YAV-8B HARRIER ▼

McDonnell Douglas YAV-8B, NAS Patuxent River, Maryland, 1979.
Two AV-8As were modified to serve as the YAV-8B prototypes, featuring a new wing, engine nozzles and other modifications to test the AV-8B configuration.

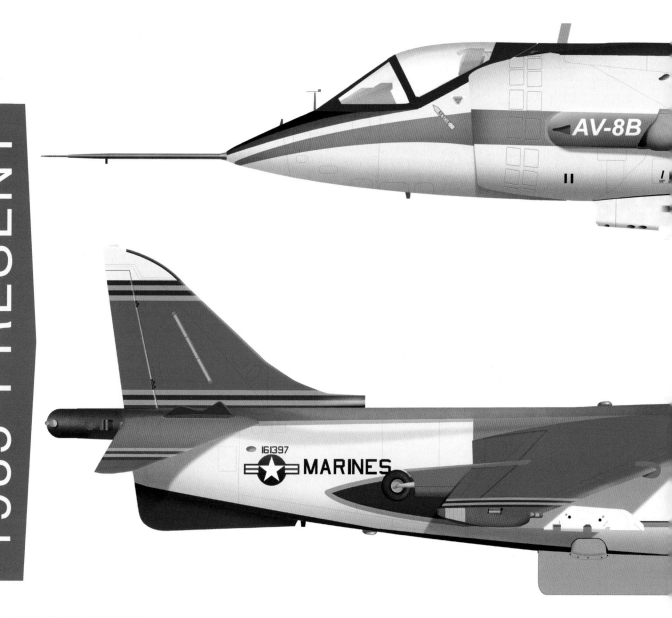

1985–PRESENT

Having forged an Anglo-American partnership for production of the AV-8A, Hawker Siddeley and McDonnell Douglas began to examine ways of addressing the type's known shortcomings – particularly its limited range and payload carrying capability. This led to plans for an Advanced Harrier.

The project was dubbed 'AV-16A' by McDonnell Douglas, while Hawker Siddeley knew it as the HS.1185. Work commenced in 1973 and focused on the Rolls-Royce Pegasus 15 engine with 24,500lb of thrust. The aircraft built around this, while retaining the original Harrier's silhouette, would have been slightly wider to accommodate the new engine as well as requiring bigger intakes and stronger nozzles.

The type would also have had longer wings of greater surface area – allowing three hardpoints per wing – plus a beefed-up undercarriage to cope with the extra weight. The cockpit would be slightly raised for better all-round visibility and a lengthened nosecone would provide sufficient space for a radar system.

At one point the USMC was discussing plans to buy a fleet of 342 AV-16As and dates were being set to fly the first prototype in 1977 when, in March 1975, the British government withdrew its support for the aircraft. Alone, the USMC could no longer justify the cost of an entirely new aircraft and the AV-16 was dropped.

However, Hawker Siddeley continued to look at how the Harrier could be improved while retaining the AV-8A's Pegasus 11 engine. Furthermore, it was discovered that through the use of a 12-degree ramp – a short rolling take-off rather than a pure vertical take-off – the original unchanged AV-8A could be made to carry the same loads projected for the AV-16A.

McDonnell Douglas, meanwhile, concentrated on the existing Harrier's structure. It was realised that major components of this subsonic aircraft could be made from lightweight carbon fibre composites, rather than metal alloys, for huge weight savings. In particular, a redesigned wing could be constructed to accommodate 2000lb of additional fuel without increasing the weight of the original aircraft.

Furthermore, careful modifications to the existing engine intakes and exhaust nozzles freed up some 600lb of additional thrust from the existing engine. And simple fixed structural devices would concentrate the engine's thrust to allow additional payload capacity during vertical take-offs. Wing sweepback was reduced,

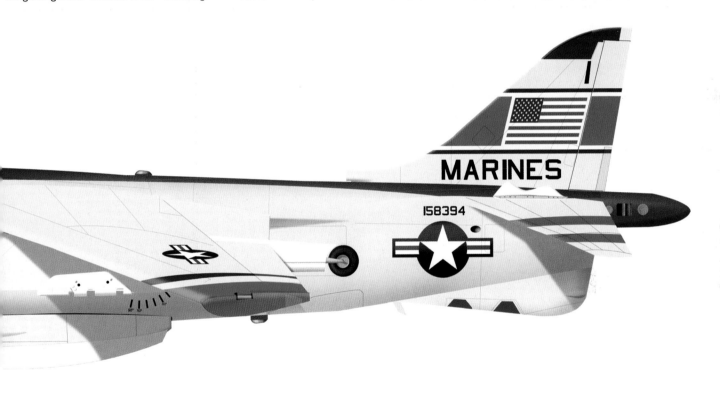

▼ MCDONNELL DOUGLAS AV-8B HARRIER

McDonnell Douglas AV-8B Harrier II, Edwards Air Force Base, California, 1983.
This is the second AV-8B Harrier II Full Scale Development aircraft. It differed from the first, which made its flight debut in 1981, in several aspects including the installation of leading edge root extensions.

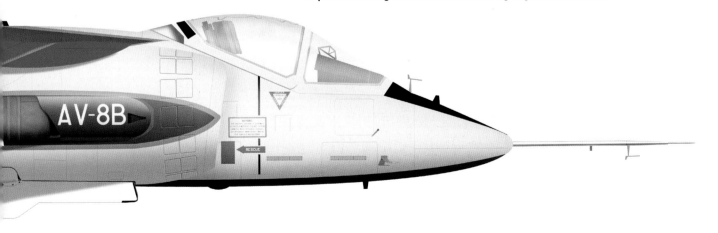

MCDONNELL DOUGLAS AV-8B HARRIER ▽

McDonnell Douglas AV-8B Harrier, Edwards Air Force Base, California, 1984.
One of the Harrier II FSD aircraft was used for stability and control tests with a parachute installation on the rear fuselage.

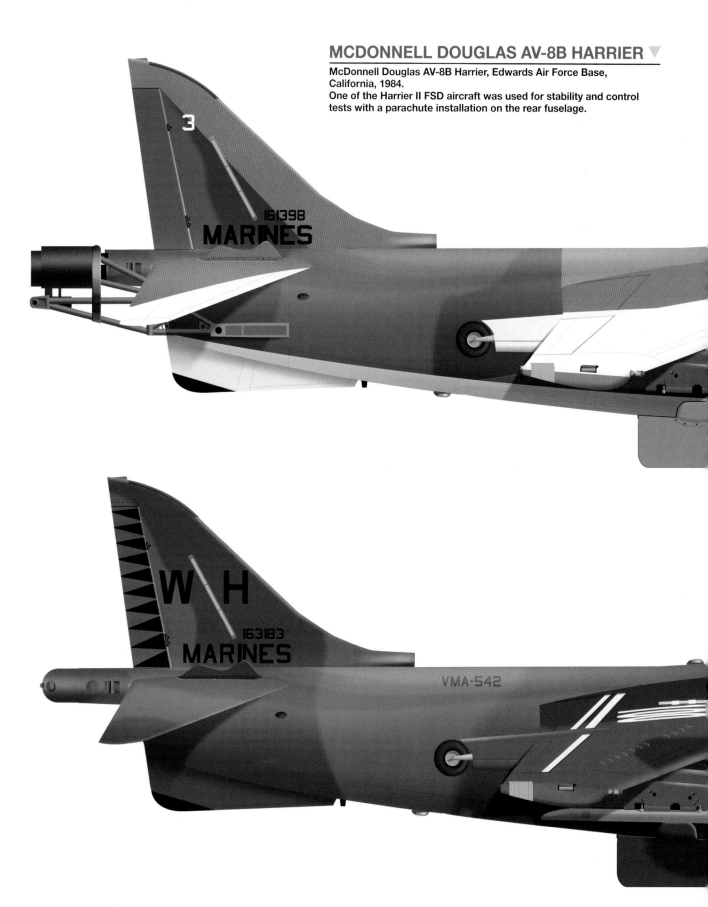

improving longitudinal stability, the wings were lengthened by 20% – as had been planned for the AV-16A – and the wingtip wheels were moved inboard to allow a tighter turning circle on the ground.

The last two AV-8As constructed by Hawker Siddeley were acquired and fitted with McDonnell Douglas's new wing to become the first YAV-8B prototypes and the first of these to be completed flew from the company's St Louis facility on November 9, 1979.

The US Navy tested the 12-degree ramp concept but the USMC, unlike the British Royal Navy, decided not to take this any further. Nevertheless, the USMC indicated a desire to buy 336 AV-8Bs to replace its existing AV-8A and A-4M Skyhawk fleets. McDonnell Douglas and Hawker Siddeley's successor, British Aerospace, signed an agreement in 1981 to divide up the manufacturing responsibilities and a

similar deal for the necessary Pegasus engines was worked out between Rolls-Royce and Pratt & Whitney.

The next step was the construction from scratch of four new Full-Scale Development (FSD) AV-8Bs, the first of which made its flight debut on November 5, 1981. The second and third FSD aircraft had wing leading edge root extensions fitted, which improved their manoeuvrability. The wing trailing edge flaps were altered for the same reason while test flights indicated that a redesign of the engine intakes would be required.

The first 16 AV-8Bs (the four FSD examples plus the first dozen production models) were powered by the F402-44-404A engine with 21,450lb of thrust. Later models, up to 1990, were fitted with the improved F402-44-406A, with the same thrust. Marine Attack Training Squadron 203 (VMAT-203) at Cherry Point took delivery of the first production Harrier II on December 12,

1983, and a period of operational evaluation (OPEVAL) commenced on August 31, 1984, which continued until March 30, 1985.

During this time, four Marine pilots put the aircraft through its paces in a variety of different potential combat conditions. The first and longest phase of OPEVAL, up to February 1, involved the AV-8B flying close air support missions – requiring action against hostile targets and coordination with friendly ground forces – in cooperation with other air support aircraft. It also assessed the aircraft's potential flying armed reconnaissance and battlefield interdiction missions.

The much shorter second phase saw the AV-8B operated as a fighter escort, flying combat air patrol and launching from the decks of vessels out at sea. OPEVAL was deemed a success and the aircraft reached initial operating capability in January 1985 with VMA-331.

▼ MCDONNELL DOUGLAS AV-8B HARRIER

McDonnell Douglas AV-8B Harrier, VMA-542, USS *John F. Kennedy* (CV-67), 1988.
The 100th AV-8B was delivered in 1988 and wore appropriate markings during tests aboard the USS *JFK*.

▼ MCDONNELL DOUGLAS AV-8B HARRIER

McDonnell Douglas AV-8B Harrier, WL-02, VMA-311, King Abdul Aziz Naval Base, Saudi Arabia, 1990.
VMA-311's AV-8Bs deployed to Saudi Arabia for Operation Desert Shield. This one is seen in ferry configuration while travelling to the Middle East in early August 1990. On January 17, 1991, VMA-311 became the first Marine squadron to employ the AV-8B in combat – hitting Iraqi positions in southern Kuwait in preparation for the coalition ground offensive.

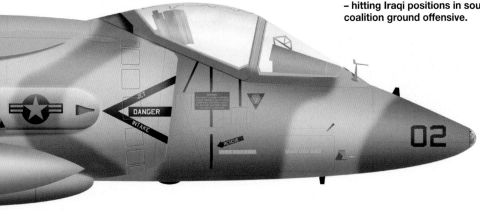

▼ MCDONNELL DOUGLAS AV-8B HARRIER

McDonnell Douglas AV-8B Harrier, WE-07, VMA-214, MCAS Yuma, Arizona, 1989.
The Night Attack (NA) variant of the AV-8B had a more powerful engine, upgraded cockpit (compatible with night-vision goggles) and a forward-looking infrared sensor housed in front of the cockpit canopy. VMA-214 was the first USMC unit equipped with this variant.

▼ BOEING/MCDONNELL DOUGLAS AV-8B HARRIER

Boeing/McDonnell Douglas AV-8B Harrier, CG-33, VMA-231, MCAS Cherry Point, North Carolina, 2002.
Several colour schemes were used for USMC AV-8Bs. This VMA-231 aircraft is overall medium grey with a mid-fuselage/upper wing pattern of dark grey.

During the trials, however, it soon became clear that the aircraft had significantly different flight characteristics to those of the AV-8A – which meant extra training was required even for experienced Harrier pilots. Within a few months, funds that would have paid for eight AV-8Bs were transferred to pay for the development of a two-seater TAV-8B trainer instead. One of these would be flown for the first time on October 21, 1986, and would be delivered to VMAT-203 on July 24, 1987.

The TAV-8B's two seats were positioned in tandem, with the fuselage extended by 3ft 11in to make this possible. The longer fuselage meant a small loss of directional stability, so the

type's fin was enlarged to compensate. The TAV-8B had only two external hardpoints and was not combat capable.

Interest from potential export customers Italy, Japan and Brazil encouraged the two partners, McDonnell Douglas and British Aerospace, to continue development of the Harrier II and the USMC was interested in a night attack variant. The result was the 87th production AV-8B, built in June 1987, being fitted with equipment for night attack. This led to a series of 66 AV-8B(NA)s being built for the USMC, with the first example delivered in September 1989.

The AV-8B(NA) differed from the standard AV-8B in having a Forward

Looking Infrared (FLIR) camera mounted on the top of its nose cone – allowing the aircraft's systems to identify objects from their heat signature using thermal imaging. It also had provision for night vision goggles, a Smiths Industries HUD and a digital moving map system supplied by Honeywell.

From 1990, AV-8Bs were retrofitted with the new F402-44-408 engine, providing 23,000lb-ft of thrust, but the new AV-8B(NA)s came with this new powerplant factory fitted. Other changes for the AV-8B(NA) included the flare and chaff dispensers being relocated and the ram air intake at the base of the fin being lengthened.

BOEING/MCDONNELL DOUGLAS AV-8B HARRIER ▽

**Boeing/McDonnell Douglas AV-8B Harrier, EH-55, VMA-542, USS *Wasp* (LHD-1), 2016.
This VMA-542 aircraft has accumulated an impressive tally of mission markings, having been heavily involved in operations.**

BOEING/MCDONNELL DOUGLAS AV-8B HARRIER ▼

Boeing/McDonnell Douglas AV-8B Harrier, KD-20, VMAT-203, MCAS Cherry Point,
North Carolina, 2014.
VMAT-203 trains AV-8B crews for the USMC using both twin- and single-seat aircraft.

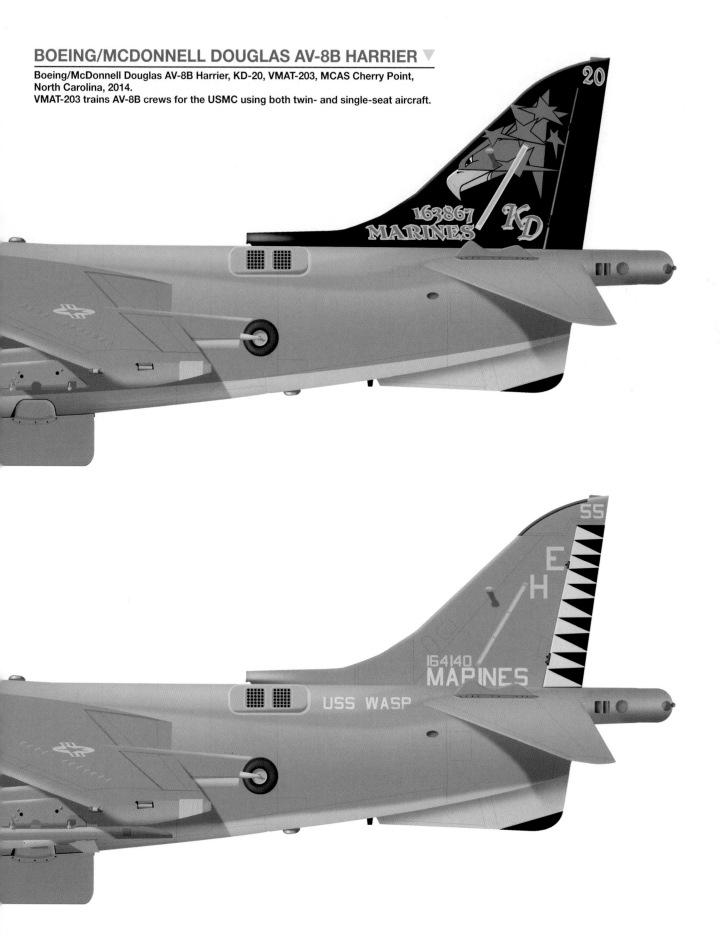

BOEING/MCDONNELL DOUGLAS AV-8B HARRIER ▼

Boeing/McDonnell Douglas AV-8B Harrier, WP-12, VMA-223, NAS Key West, Florida, 2015.
The AV-8B Plus variant introduced the APG-65 radar, greatly improving air-to-air capability. This example carries a typical air-to-air load of Sidewinders and Slammers in addition to a gun pod.

BOEING/MCDONNELL DOUGLAS AV-8B HARRIER ▼

Boeing/McDonnell Douglas AV-8B Harrier, EG-50, VMA-231, USS *Bataan* (LHD-5), 2014.
USMC AV-8Bs can be deployed as part of composite expeditionary formations. For example, this Harrier from VMA-231 was integrated into Marine Medium Tiltrotor Squadron (VMM) 263 as part of the 22nd Marine Expeditionary Unit (MEU). AV-8Bs can carry four external fuel tanks for ferry flights.

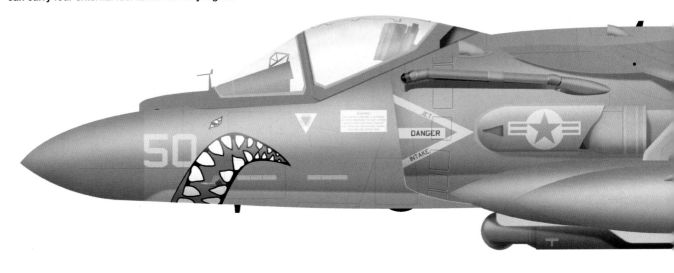

Even as work was commencing on the first AV-8B(NA), back in June 1987, McDonnell Douglas and British Aerospace were launching a private venture to further upgrade the basic AV-8B's systems as the AV-8B Plus. This would incorporate many of the AV-8B(NA)'s features but with the addition of the APG-65 multi-mode pulse-Doppler radar housed in an extended nose cone. Plenty of these systems were available, having recently been removed from early F/A-18s, and would allow the Harrier II to carry advanced missiles – particularly the AIM-120 AMRAAM but also the AGM-65 Maverick and McDonnell Douglas's own Harpoon.

Eventually both Italy and Spain joined the USMC in purchasing the AV-8B Plus – with the US Navy acting as an agent for all three. The USMC agreed to purchase 30 new aircraft, with 72 older AV-8Bs being rebuilt to Plus standard. A prototype of the new variant took its first flight on September 22, 1992, while the earliest production example first flew on March 17, 1993.

The first four older AV-8Bs were rebuilt during the 1994 financial year and the first was delivered to the USMC in January 1996. The last of the 72 rebuilds was delivered in December 2003.

Arguably the USMC Harrier II's finest hour would be its participation in the Gulf War of 1990-1991. By the time Iraqi forces invaded Kuwait on August 2, 1990, the Marine Corps had six operational AV-8B day attack squadrons equipped with 20 aircraft each. There was also a single large Harrier II training unit and two further squadrons, VMA-211 and VMA-214, were in the midst of transitioning from the A-4M to the AV-8B(NA).

On August 11, the Marine Corps deployed I Marine Expeditionary Force to the Persian Gulf, including the 3rd Marine Aircraft Wing – which itself included the Harrier IIs of MAG-13 – Marine Air Group 13. Following five months of build-up, Operation Desert Storm commenced on January 17. The

first Marine Corps aircraft in operation were F/A-18s and A-6Es – the Harrier II units initially had their missions cancelled due to a lack of EA-6Bs to provide electronic warfare support.

However, shortly after dawn on the opening day of the attack, an OV-10 Bronco spotted an Iraqi artillery position shelling Marines near al-Khafji, a Saudi town 9.6km south of the Kuwaiti border. Subsequently, four AV-8Bs of VMA-311 carrying 1000lb bombs were launched from King Abdulaziz Air Base in Saudi Arabia with Major Terry C Branch, the squadron's executive officer, in command. The Harriers dive-bombed and strafed the Iraqi position and the

crew of the OV-10 reported seeing artillery tubes tumbling through the air.

After that first day, the Marine AV-8Bs became, according to the commander of MAG-13 Colonel John R Bioty Jr, "very much a part of the war" and southern Kuwait became a "Harrier hunting ground". The Harrier units' main objective was to support the troops by destroying as many Iraqi troop, vehicle and equipment targets as possible.

AV-8B pilots attacking with unguided bombs usually initiated their dive at 30,000ft at an angle of between 45 and 60-degrees, releasing their ordnance at 10,000ft. They also found that their 25mm cannon could be devastatingly effective.

Iraqi anti-aircraft fire and SAMs remained a serious threat at low altitudes throughout the campaign, with five AV-8Bs being lost and two Marine pilots killed – Captain James N Wilbourn and Captain Reginald C Underwood.

While the AV-8B was fast and manoeuvrable, it also proved highly vulnerable to battle damage – having only one engine and with many vital components positioned around it in the centre of the aircraft. Even a near miss from a heat-seeking missile could prove fatal. Underwood's AV-8B was hit by anti-aircraft fire during an attack on targets in Northern Kuwait and he was killed in the ensuing crash.

BOEING/MCDONNELL DOUGLAS AV-8B HARRIER ▽

Boeing/McDonnell Douglas AV-8B Harrier, CF-01, VMA-211, 2015.
This USMC AV-8B was deployed during Operation Inherent Resolve – the
international intervention in Syria. VMA-211 aircraft operated both from land bases
and from aboard amphibious assault ships.

MCDONNELL DOUGLAS TAV-8B HARRIER ▽

McDonnell Douglas TAV-8B Harrier, SD-626, NATC, Patuxent River,
Maryland, 1988.
During testing at the Naval Air Warfare Center, this TAV-8B was painted
with the initial land camouflage colour scheme.

MCDONNELL DOUGLAS AV-8B HARRIER

McDonnell Douglas AV-8B Harrier, VL-05, VMA-331, USS *Nassau* (LHA-4), 1991.
Almost all Harriers involved in Desert Storm were painted in new colour schemes consisting of two shades of grey; there was a lot of colour variation between squadrons however and even between aircraft of the same squadron.

VMA-542 pilot John S Walsh had an extremely close call when his AV-8B was hit by a SAM as he attacked an Iraqi armoured column. He was about 8000ft up and the infrared-guided missile struck the aircraft amidships, perforating the right wing, blowing off the flap and setting fire to the fuel in the wing tank.

Trailing fire from the blazing tank, Walsh tried to reach Ahmad al-Jaber Air Base in Kuwait, which had just fallen to the Marines. Hovering 900ft above the ground, the pilot tried to extend his landing gear but it wouldn't budge. As Walsh looked for the best place to eject, the aircraft's controls abruptly froze and it flipped onto its back. Having ejected, the seat saved Walsh's life just in time and he was rescued by a Marine patrol.

Nevertheless, the Marines found that the Harrier possessed attributes which made it invaluable during the 43 days of Desert Storm. Stationed at the forward base of Ras at-Tanajib, Harriers needed only a fraction of the 10,000ft runway to take off. On returning, they could land vertically and taxi a short distance to the refuelling and rearming area. Pilots would grab a bite to eat, drink some water, visit the restroom then get back in the cockpit ready for another mission.

During Operations Desert Shield – the five month build-up – and Desert Storm combined, the Marines' AV-8B fleet made 3380 flights with 4083 flight hours. Mission availability was over 90%. And after the war, between 1992 and 2003, USMC AV-8Bs flew patrols over Iraqi as part of Operation Southern Watch.

Throughout the 1990s and early 2000s, AV-8Bs provided air cover and armed reconnaissance during numerous international operations – including Rwanda in 1994, Liberia in 1996 and 2003, the Central African Republic in 1996, Albania, Sierra Leone and Zaire in 1997 and East Timor in 2002. In 1999, 12 Harrier IIs participated in the NATO mission Operation Allied Force in Yugoslavia, flying 34 combat air support missions against targets in Kosovo from USS *Nassau*.

AV-8Bs and AV-8B(NA)s also took part in Operation Enduring Freedom in Afghanistan, starting in 2001. Six AV-8B(NA)s from VMA-513 were deployed to Bagram Air Base in October 2002 and carried out reconnaissance and attack missions primarily at night using the LITENING targeting pod.

The early stages of Operation Iraqi Freedom in 2003 saw 60 AV-8Bs deployed on vessels including the USS *Bonhomme Richard* and USS *Bataan*. In just under a month of combat, more than 2000 sorties were flown to provide Marine Corps ground forces with 24-hour support. However, the AV-8B drew criticism for its limited ability to remain on station – only 15-20 minutes in some instances. During the heavy fighting in and around the stronghold of Fallujah in 2004, AV-8Bs were used in combination with artillery to provide precision fire support for Marine forces operating in the urban environment.

Harrier IIs launched from USS *Kearsarge* helped to enforce the UN no-fly zone over Libya during Operation Odyssey Dawn, from March 20, 2011 – including one instance where several AV-8Bs defended the pilot of a downed F-15E from approaching Libyans prior to his extraction aboard an MV-22 Osprey.

The USN bought the UK's fleet of 72 retired Harrier IIs – 63 GR.7s, GR.9s and GR.9As, plus nine two-seater T.12/12As – for $180 million in November 2011 to provide a source of cheap spaces for the Marine Corps. And on September 14, 2012, six AV-8Bs belonging to VMA-211 were destroyed and another two were severely damaged during a Taliban raid on

Camp Bastion in Afghanistan's Helmand Province. The squadron's commander, Lieutenant Colonel Chris Raible was killed while leading a counterattack on the Afghan infiltrators armed only with a pistol.

It was announced in June 2013 that the Harrier II, which had been scheduled for retirement in 2015, would remain active until 2030, with wind-down only commencing in 2027. However, the following year it was decided that the aircraft's retirement would be brought forward to 2025 to allow a period of overlap with its replacement, the F-35, which was due to enter service in 2015.

In November 2015, Marine Corps AV-8Bs launched from USS *Kearsarge*

flew strike missions against Islamic State forces in Iraq. And in June 2016, AV-8Bs of the 13th MEU, flying from USS *Boxer* in the Persian Gulf, conducted airstrikes against Islamic State positions in Syria as part of Operation Inherent Resolve.

April 2021 saw the US Department of the Navy back-pedalling once again on the Harrier's retirement, awarding Vertex Aerospace a $123 million contract to keep the USMC's AV-8Bs in service until 2029, with BAE Systems as subcontractor. At the time of writing, the Marine Corps inventory consisted of 124 active Harrier IIs – 74 AV-8Bs, 16 TAV-8Bs and 34 AV-8B(NA)s – split between five squadrons.

BOEING/MCDONNELL DOUGLAS TAV-8B HARRIER ▼

Boeing/McDonnell Douglas TAV-8B Harrier, KD-02, VMAT-203, MCAS Cherry Point, North Carolina, 2012.
The dual-seat TAV-8B is used for training including weapons delivery; this aircraft carries a triple ejector rack with MK.76 practice bombs.

BOEING/MCDONNELL DOUGLAS AV-8B HARRIER ▼

Boeing/McDonnell Douglas AV-8B Harrier, WF-01, VMA-513, Eielson Air Force Base, Alaska, 2007.
A Harrier from VMA-513 Flying Nightmares had special fin art added for deployment to the 2007 Red Flag Alaska exercise.

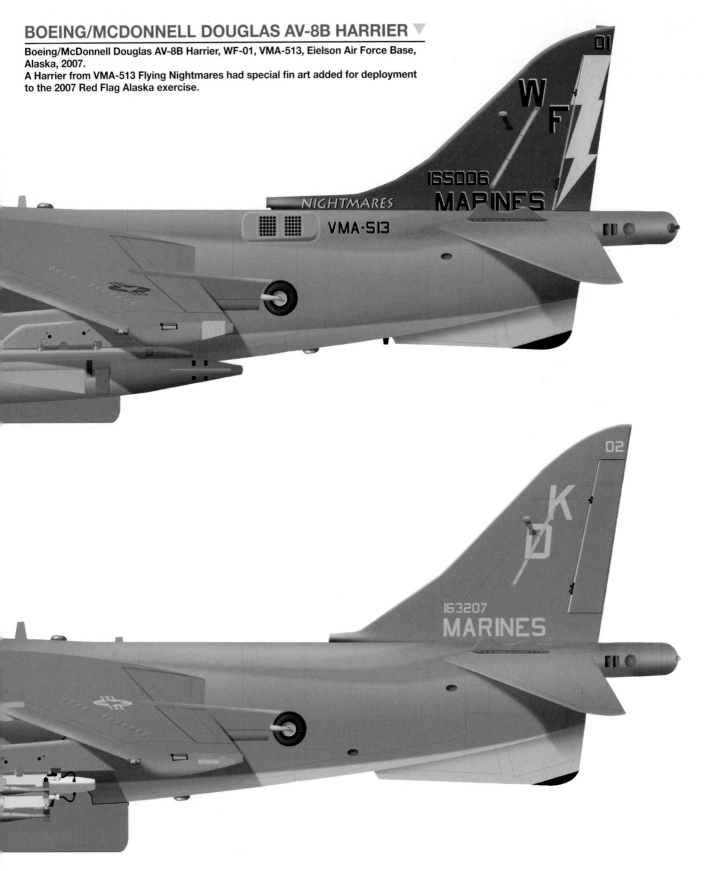

LOCKHEED MARTIN F-35 LIGHTNING II

The Marine Corps operates both the F-35B and F-35C variants of the Lightning II strike fighter – the only force anywhere in the world to do so. The fifth-generation F-35 is at the cutting edge of stealth and electronics technology but whether its flight performance and real-world combat abilities are up to scratch remains to be seen.

LOCKHEED MARTIN F-35B LIGHTNING II ▼

Lockheed Martin F-35B Lightning II, BF-01, NAS Patuxent River, Maryland, 2008.
The first F-35B began its flight test programme in 2008.

2019–PRESENT

LOCKHEED MARTIN F-35B LIGHTNING II ▼

Lockheed Martin F-35B Lightning II, BF-02, USS *Wasp* (LHD-1), 2011.
The second VTOL Lightning II went supersonic in June 2010; it also performed the type's first vertical ship landings on the USS *Wasp*.

The origin of the USMC's involvement in the F-35 programme can be traced back to 1993 and the commencement of the DARPA Common Affordable Lightweight Fighter (CALF) project. This was intended to create a VSTOL strike fighter able to replace the Harrier IIs of both the Marine Corps and the British Royal Navy – with the potential, it was hoped, to also provide the USAF with a new low-cost high-tech fighter.

In 1994, less than a year into CALF, Congress decided that the Marine effort should be merged with the parallel Joint Advanced Strike Technology (JAST) programme being run by the USAF and USN in order to avoid the higher cost of developing, procuring, operating and supporting three separate tactical aircraft designs.

McDonnell Douglas, Northrop Grumman, Lockheed Martin and Boeing had already submitted design studies for JAST in 1993 and with the absorption of CALF the programme was renamed Joint Strike Fighter (JSF) in 1994. It was optimistically believed at this time that a strike aircraft could be designed and built which could meet the requirements of all three American services – the Marine Corps, Air Force and Navy – and potentially those of many foreign air forces too.

Given the many different roles that this aircraft would be called upon to fulfil, it was envisioned even at this early stage that three variants would be required: one with conventional take-off and landing, another with VSTOL capability and a dedicated carrier version for catapult assisted take-off. These would, however, have a high parts commonality and the differences between them would be kept to a minimum.

Despite the emphasis on strike and close-support, the new aircraft would also be able to operate in the air supremacy role if required. It was certainly an ambitious project and having already been involved in CALF with the Marines, and still requiring a Harrier II replacement, the UK agreed to buy in as a top-tier partner on JSF in November 1995.

Submissions for JSF were received from McDonnell Douglas (teamed with Northrop Grumman and British Aerospace), Lockheed Martin and Boeing and on November 16, 1996, both Lockheed Martin and Boeing received $750 million contracts to develop prototypes.

The design being developed by the former received the designation X-35 while the latter's became the X-32. Two X-35 prototypes were developed – the conventional take-off X-35A, which would later be refitted to become the VSTOL X-35B, and the X-35C, which had larger wings.

When it emerged in 2000 it was clear that the design of the original X-35A prototype was influenced by Lockheed Martin's F-22 design, which at this point was still five years away from entering service with the USAF. It made its debut flight on October 24, 2000, and less than a month later, on November 22, 2000, the process of converting it into the X-35B began. The second prototype, the X-35C, took its first flight on December 16, 2000.

The fly-off between the X-35 and Boeing's X-32 took place in early-to-mid 2001, during which the X-35B was able to take off in less than 500ft, go supersonic, then land vertically – which the X-32 was unable to match.

LOCKHEED MARTIN F-35B LIGHTNING II ▼

Lockheed Martin F-35B Lightning II, VK-01, VMFA-121, MCAS Iwakuni, Japan, 2017.
VMFA-121 was the first permanently forward deployed F-35B squadron of the USMC.

On October 26, 2001, Lockheed Martin was declared the winner and awarded a contract for system development and demonstration. By now the JSF programme was being funded jointly by the US, UK, Italy, Holland, Canada, Turkey, Australia, Norway and Denmark.

Lockheed Martin enlarged the X-35 somewhat during the process of turning it into the basis for a production-ready design, the forward fuselage being stretched by 5in to provide extra room for the avionics bay. The tailplanes were correspondingly moved 2in further to the rear in order to retain balance. The upper fuselage was raised by an inch along the centre line as well. Parts manufacture for the first prototype F-35 began on November 10, 2003.

LOCKHEED MARTIN F-35B LIGHTNING II ▼

Lockheed Martin F-35B Lightning II, MX-52, VMX-1, Edwards Air Force Base, California, 2016.
This F-35B from test squadron VMX-1 shows off its weapons bay during operational tests of the AIM-120 AMRAAM.

A key issue with the X-35 prototypes had been their lack of an internal weapons bay – which would become a requirement for the production model. As such, numerous design changes were necessary and the aircraft's weight grew by a not-inconsiderable 2200lb. In order to compensate, Lockheed Martin increased engine power, thinned down the airframe members, reduced the size of the space originally projected for the weapons bay itself and slimmed down the aircraft's fins. The electrical system was also altered, as was the portion of the aircraft just behind the cockpit. Taken together, these measures succeeded in reducing weight by 2700lb. The cost, however, was $6.2 billion and making the changes had eaten up 18 months of development time.

The Marine Corps had the option, at one stage, of procuring the F/A-18E/F as its next strike fighter but opted instead to wait for the F-35 – with plans in place to procure 353 F-35Bs and 67 F-35Cs.

LOCKHEED MARTIN F-35B LIGHTNING II ▼

Lockheed Martin F-35B Lightning II, DC-01, VMFA-122, MCAS Yuma, Arizona, 2018.
F-35Bs can carry external loads when stealth is not required – as demonstrated by this VMFA-122 aircraft.

Powered by a single Pratt & Whitney F135-PW-600 engine with 40,000lb-ft of thrust – derived from the F-22's F119 engine – a fully loaded Marine Corps F-35B can fly at Mach 1.2 for 150 miles without using its afterburner. With afterburner, it has a top speed of Mach 1.6. The aircraft measures 51.2ft long and 14.3ft high with a wingspan of 35ft and a wing area of 460ft^2. Its empty weight is 32,300lb, fuel capacity is 13,500lb and maximum weapons payload is 15,000lb.

Standard internal weapons load is two AIM-120C/D air-to-air missiles plus two 1000lb GBU-32 JDAM guided bombs. Combat radius is 450nm and range on internal fuel alone is 900nm. Its maximum G-rating is 7.0.

The Marine Corps F-35C has a slightly different engine – the F135-PW-100 – but output is the same at 40,000lb-ft thrust and top speed is the same as that of the F-35B. The aircraft's dimensions are also different; it is 3in longer than the

LOCKHEED MARTIN F-35B LIGHTNING II ▼

Lockheed Martin F-35B Lightning II, WF-502, VMFAT-502, MCAS Beaufort, South Carolina, 2020.
Marine Fighter Attack Squadron VMFAT-502 received its first F-35B in 2020 alongside VMFAT-501.

LOCKHEED MARTIN F-35B LIGHTNING II ▽

Lockheed Martin F-35B Lightning II, VM-51, VMFAT-501, MCAS Beaufort, South Carolina, 2018.
Contrasting with the usual rather dull external appearance of fifth-generation fighters, this F-35B from VMFAT-501 displays full-colour markings.

LOCKHEED MARTIN F-35B LIGHTNING II

Lockheed Martin F-35B Lightning II, DC-122, VMFA-122, MCAS Yuma, Arizona, 2020.
Without a built-in gun, the F-35B relies on a gun pod mounted ventrally.

LOCKHEED MARTIN F-35C LIGHTNING II

Lockheed Martin F-35C Lightning II, VW-434, VMFA-314, MCAS Miramar, California, 2020.
The USMC procured the carrier-capable F-35C alongside the VTOL F-35B. The first USMC F-35C squadron to achieved operational status was VMFA-314.

F-35B at 51.5ft and 4in taller at 14.7ft. Its wingspan is 8ft wider at 43ft and wing area, understandably for a carrier aircraft, is much greater at 668ft^2. Empty, it weighs 2500lb more at 34,800lb, fuel capacity is 6250lb more than that of the F-35B at 19,750lb and weapons payload too is greater at 18,000lb.

Standard internal weapons load for the Marine F-35C is two AIM-120C/D plus two 2000lb GBU-31 JDAM guided bombs.

Combat radius on internal fuel is 600nm and range is 1200nm. Maximum G-rating is slightly higher than that of the F-35B at 7.5.

Neither aircraft has the internal 25mm GAU-22/A cannon of the F-35A, but both have the option to carry it externally as a pod with 220 rounds if required. Four underwing pylons can carry additional AIM-120s, AGM-158 cruise missiles and guided bombs. Two further near-wingtip pylons are designed for the AIM-9X

▼ LOCKHEED MARTIN F-35B LIGHTNING II

Lockheed Martin F-35B Lightning II, CF-01, VMFA-211, USS *America* (LHA-6), 2016.
F-35Bs of the USMC are intended to operate from amphibious assault ships such as USS *America*.

▼ LOCKHEED MARTIN F-35C LIGHTNING II

Lockheed Martin F-35C Lightning II, NJ-123, VFA-101, USS *George Washington* (CVN-73), 2016.
USMC F-35C crews are trained by VFA-101, a squadron operating with aircraft and personnel from both the US Navy and USMC.

sidewinder and AIM-132 ASRAAM. Using both internal and external stations an air-to-air missile load of eight AIM-120s and two AIM-9s is possible.

Inside its cockpit, the F-35 has a 20x8in touchscreen, a speech-recognition system, a helmet-mounted display, a right-hand side stick controller,

a Martin-Baker ejection seat and an oxygen generation system derived from that of the F-22. Due to the helmet display, the aircraft does not have a HUD. Its radar is the AN/APG-81 developed by Northrop Grumman Electronic Systems with the addition of the nose-mounted Electro-Optical

Targeting System. The F-35's electronic warfare suite is the AN/ASQ-239 (Barracuda) with sensor fusion of radio frequency and infrared tracking, advanced radar warning receiver including geolocation of targeting of threats, and multispectral image countermeasures.

The aircraft has 10 radio frequency antennas embedded in its wings and tail. Six passive infrared sensors are distributed across the F-35 as part of Northrop Grumman's AN/AAQ-37 distributed aperture system. This provides missile warning, reports missile launch locations, detects and tracks approaching aircraft and replaces traditional night vision devices.

The first F-35, AA-1, was rolled out on February 20, 2006, and the type was formally given the name Lightning II on July 7, 2006 – the 'II' making it a spiritual successor to both the Lockheed P-38 Lightning of the USAAF during

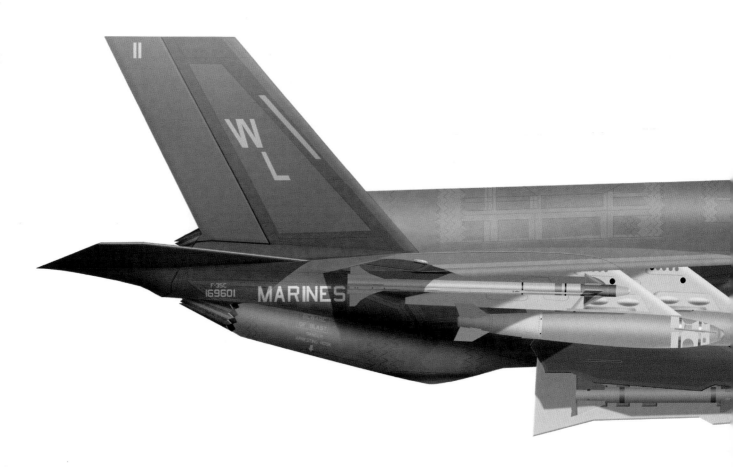

the Second World War and the British English Electric Lightning of the Cold War. AA-1 made its flight debut on December 15, 2006.

The first F-35B made its flight debut on June 11, 2008, with its first hover taking place on March 17, 2010. Its first vertical landing took place the day after. The F-35C took its first flight on June 6, 2010.

Marine Fighter Attack Squadron 121 conducted its first operational F-35B flight at Marine Corps Air Station Yuma,

Arizona, on February 21, 2013, and the following month sea trials were carried out on amphibious assault ship USS *Wasp*. Trials would continue throughout 2013.

All US F-35s were grounded in 2014 following a runway fire incident involving an F-35A at Eglin Air Force Base on June 23. The following month, the flight ban was lifted and testing of the USMC's F-35Bs resumed. Marine Operational and Evaluation Squadron 22 (VMX-22) received its first F-35B for operational

testing and evaluation at Edwards Air Force Base, California, on October 9, 2014. From March to May 2015, Marine Fighter Attack Training Squadron 501 – the Marine Corps F-35B training squadron – conducted a series of night flying trials with the type, and on July 31, 2015, the Marine Corps declared F-35B Initial Operational Capability.

The USMC lost its first Lightning II when an F-35B burst into flames in flight on October 27, 2016, forcing the pilot

▼ LOCKHEED MARTIN F-35B LIGHTNING II

Lockheed-Martin F-35B Lightning II, DT-02, VMFA-242, MCAS Iwakuni, Japan, 2020.
As usual with USMC aircraft, the F-35B uses the probe and drogue refuelling system. It carries a retractable probe on the right front fuselage.

▼ LOCKHEED MARTIN F-35C LIGHTNING II

Lockheed-Martin F-35C Lightning II, WL-11, VMFA-311, MCAS Miramar, California, 2022.
Carrying additional weapons externally can increase the F-35C's offensive power at the expense of its full stealth capabilities. VMFA-311 was due to be reactivated in 2022, flying the F-35C.

to make an emergency landing at Marine Corps Air Station Beaufort, South Carolina.

The first Marine F-35C squadron, VMFA-314, began to receive them on January 21, 2020, at MCAS Miramar, its pilots having begun training with the US Navy's F-35C Fleet Replacement Squadron VFA-125 in September 2019. Finally, in December 2020, VMFA-314 achieved Initial Operational Capability on the F-35C.

Over the years the F-35 programme has struggled with delays, cost overruns and even accusations of industrial espionage. Critics have pointed to the aircraft's apparently lacklustre performance – slower and less manoeuvrable than some of the aircraft it is intended to replace – and questions over its ability to effectively combat the new fifth-generation types appearing abroad, such as the Russian Sukhoi Su-57 and the Chinese J20.

There have also been worries about gaps in its stealth coating, engine issues, symptoms of oxygen starvation reported by some pilots, and of course the highly-publicised mid-air fires.

Then again, whenever F-35s have taken part in large scale air combat training exercises they have performed well. During the Red Flag 19-2 exercises in 2019, five F-35As flown by the Italian Air Force achieved outstanding results – on average seven SAM systems and five 'enemy' air assets were killed during each mission for no losses, with 100% availability of the aircraft on each day.

One Italian officer commented: "We knew we had an operational advantage, due to the fifth generation technology, but we didn't expect such a high 'kill' ratio: in the 16 Offensive Counter Air missions we flew, we neutralised more than 100 SAM systems and never lost a plane."

Two years earlier, during Red Flag 17-1, USMC F-35Bs facing Dutch F-16s managed a 'kill' ratio of 20-1 on average – even achieving 24-0 in one exercise. And this was with the F-35s configured for strike missions rather than air superiority.

The F-35B and F-35C are only just beginning their careers as front line combat aircraft with the Marine Corps and it remains to be seen just how they will fare against the new challenges certain to arise over the coming years.

LOCKHEED MARTIN F-35C LIGHTNING II ▽

Lockheed-Martin F-35C Lightning II, VMFAT-401, MCAS Yuma, Arizona, 2030.
This speculative image shows a USMC F-35C being operated in the adversary role.